Lead Me Out to the Ballgame

Lead Me Out to the Ballgame

Stories and Strategies to Develop
MAJOR LEAGUE LEADERSHIP

Howard C. Fero, PhD
Rebecca L. Herman, PhD

Major League Leadership Enterprises, LLC

Major League Leadership Enterprises, LLC
PO Box 110773
Trumbull, CT 06611
www.MajorLeaguePress.com
203-983-0983

ISBN 978-0-9960880-0-8

10 9 8 7 6 5 4 3 2 1

To all who desire to marry their passion with their work and lead with their heart, play ball!

The Starting Lineup

Acknowledgements

The research, analysis, and writing of this book were an incredible process filled with excitement as well as hard work. As lifelong baseball fans it was a great thrill to be in the clubhouses of Major League Baseball teams, and as leadership enthusiasts, it was great to hear how those who lead America's pastime go about leading their players.

Our goal of learning about how Major League Baseball managers lead their teams couldn't have been achieved without the gracious hospitality of the Major League teams who allowed us access to their clubhouses and granted us interviews with their managers and players. With that we want to first acknowledge those teams who afforded us this rare luxury of entering their sanctuaries. A big thank you to the Arizona Diamondbacks, Boston Red Sox, Cleveland Indians, Colorado Rockies, Houston Astros, Kansas City Royals, Los Angeles Angels, Los Angeles Dodgers, Milwaukee Brewers, Minnesota Twins, Oakland Athletics, Pittsburgh Pirates, San Diego Padres, San Francisco Giants, Seattle Mariners, Tampa Bay Rays, Toronto Blue Jays, and Washington Nationals. In addition to the managers and / or players from the above baseball teams we were fortunate to have met some great resources along our travels who provided us with stories and expertise from their years in the Game. Thanks so much to Jim Duquette, former General Manager of the New York Mets, former Vice President of the Baltimore Orioles and current radio personality on Sirius XM's MLB Network Radio, for sharing with us some great stories. Thanks as well to Jim's on air partner, Mike Ferrin, who also shared some great anecdotes with us. There are some great sports writers in baseball and we are very appreciative that Washington Post columnist and author Tom Boswell spent some time sharing stories with us of his time studying and writing about baseball. At the end of this manuscript you will find a roster of those people we interviewed for this book, but we'd like to take a moment here to thank a couple of MLB insiders who helped us along the way. Thanks to Red Sox pitcher and founder of the Strike 3 Foundation, Craig Breslow, for his perspective on the game (he is, as the Wall Street Journal dubbed him, the smartest guy in baseball). Craig spent time with us discussing his perspectives prior to the official start of our research and helped us to understand a bit about the goings on in a MLB clubhouse. Thanks also to Oakland A's manager Bob Melvin, who was also our first interview. Bob met us at a Starbucks and allowed us to pilot some of our interview protocol with him which helped us to fine tune the questions we took with us on our interviews.

In addition to our baseball acknowledgements we would like to thank Michelle Black Wester for transcribing our interviews. Even with her very limited knowledge of baseball she managed to spell most of the names and baseball jargon correctly! Thank you to Pamela Sparks for her patience in working with us through many iterations of our cover design. Her creative approach captured the essence of our message. Thank you also to Denise Lampman Wells for her expert editing. Her critical eye helped us to combine our voices and clarify jargon to improve our final product. Thank you as well to Dr. Jay Polmar and his team for their work on the interior layout of this book and for helping us to deliver it to you, the reader, in its current form.

A special thank you to the students in the Leadership and MBA programs at Albertus Magnus College for helping to conduct secondary research about our managers both before and after our interviews, the context you gave to our work was immensely useful. We'd also like to thank the administrations at Albertus Magnus College and Kaplan University for their support throughout our research and writing of this book.

Finally, we would like to thank our families and friends for their support, patience, and understanding during our time researching and writing.

Howard

To my wife Lisa, who encouraged me to take on this project, supported me throughout the process, and even accepted that I *had* to watch all the baseball games I attended after my interviews were completed as it would be rude to leave before the last pitch...thanks! To Ben, my pride and joy who will perhaps one day appear on a major league roster, keep following your passion as it will help lead you to success. To Saige and Zac, my young twins who have spent most of their lives watching me working on this book, follow your big brother's lead, you make me proud with who you are and who I know you will become! To my parents who supported me and gave me the confidence to follow my dreams, push through adversity, and always be true to my values and to myself, thank you, without your unconditional support through all I have tackled, I wouldn't be where I am today. Sadly, my father passed away prior to the completion of this manuscript, but I know he would be proud that the early chapters that he read turned into *Lead Me Out to the Ballgame*. Finally, thanks to my co-author, Dr. Rebecca Herman, for her friendship and her partnership. Writing with you has made this process both fun and rewarding. I will miss our weekly calls, and the support we gave to each other during this process. I look forward to the start of those again when we begin our next project!

Rebecca

To my son, Trevor, who originally ignited my love for the sport of baseball – just look what you did! Thank you for sharing this journey with me and often waiting on the sidelines (literally) while I finished an interview. I hope that your passion for the sport continues to grow and that you will also be able to unite your love of the game with a satisfying career in the future. To my parents, who always told me that I could do anything I set my mind to do. Without your support and confidence, I'm not sure I would have grown into the woman I am today and one who was confident enough to march into a Major League clubhouse to interview half-clothed men! To Wayne, who is not only my best friend but also my resident baseball expert! Thank you for being a constant source of encouragement and an amazing cheerleader. You listened to many hours of discussion about this book and the process of completing it and still want to take on a writing project with me. I am blessed by your friendship. Finally, to Howard, my co-author and friend – who knew that a hallway chat at a conference would result in a 2 ½ year project and a finished book! We complemented one another with our 'Yin and Yang' approach to things and made each other stronger – and even had fun along the way. I look forward to seeing what our *Major League Leadership* partnership will bring.

Howard and Rebecca, 2014

Pregame

You'd be surprised that even amongst veterans in baseball they're looking for leadership

Bob Melvin, manager, Oakland A's

"Strike 3 - you're out!"

"Ball 4 - take your base!"

"Out of the park...homerun!"

It's all pretty cut and dry in baseball. The umpire makes a call, and for better or worse, that's the way it is (well, maybe a review here and there!). With leadership however, rules aren't quite as clear cut...there isn't always one right call to make, there isn't always one strategy to employ, and there isn't always only one person who makes the call. Leadership is a process which, to be utilized successfully, requires an understanding of some basic tenets, or, as we call them, the *Bases of Leadership*. To be a successful leader we need to understand ourselves, our strengths and our weaknesses, understand the people we are leading, their differences and dispositions, and understand the specific situation we are in. In order to be successful at leading we need to understand that we can't lead the first game of the season with a team of rookies the same way we will lead the last game of the season with a team of veterans; and understand that no matter how good a leader we think we are, if we don't pay attention to our surroundings, our trophies can slip away.

During baseball's Spring Training in March of 2012 and 2013, and throughout the 2012 and 2013 Major League Baseball seasons, we, Drs. Howard Fero and Rebecca Herman, set out to identify the leadership techniques, attitudes, and behaviors that Major League Baseball (MLB) managers use to engage their team, build trust within their clubhouse, and create a team of champions. To do this we interviewed current and former MLB managers, current and former players, executives, and members of the media, and learned what they believe makes for a successful leader in a Major League clubhouse. Our interviews were conducted in Major League clubhouses as players prepared to take the field, in the manager's offices, and even in the dugout during pregame warm-ups. The *Lead Me Out to the Ballgame* roster stands at over 100 interviews representing players and managers from nearly two thirds of the teams in Major League Baseball.

Major League Leadership©

Common questions asked by business leaders, professors, coaches, and fans that we have met along the way were: What really makes a leader great and what are the things they need to do? When beginning a new job, aiming for a promotion, or simply looking to improve ourselves we turn to leadership. This concept is one which is used quite extensively in all parts of our life, personally and professionally, but what does it truly mean? What does it take to be a leader, and can we all be leaders in our lives? The simple answer is, it takes work to be a leader, but we can all be one in our own lives. The manner to do this, however, takes a bit of work, but in our book we aim to make that work fun as we explore the ways to develop our leadership through stories and examples of how it is cultivated in major league clubhouses. Throughout this book we will introduce to you to and explore a model of leadership which we have coined *Major League Leadership*. Through stories and examples we will tell you about the ten *Bases of Leadership* which make up our model and will recount for you some of the stories we heard during our interviews about how managers throughout baseball demonstrate these *bases* and use them to inspire their teams to achieve what is expected of them, and often surpass those expectations. This book was written for both the baseball enthusiast who will enjoy hearing about our visits with some of the icons of baseball and also for those people who want some clear and specific strategies to cultivate their leadership skills and acumen. You don't have to understand baseball to learn from the strategies of MLB managers!

As we analyzed the many interviews we conducted, one of the themes that emerged time and time again was that leading a team does not center solely on operational strategy, or as it is referred to in baseball, the "X's and O's". As will be explored, strategy and expertise are not all the ingredients needed for a successful team. Sure, the "X's and O's" are important, and just like people outside of the Game, players need to know what they need to do each day and be aware of the team's overall strategy and goals, but, as Arizona Diamondback pitcher Craig Breslow told us, "there are very few instances where you can point to managerial mistakes as crucial to the outcome of the game...more than that [the key to success] is keeping guys motivated, keeping guys competing." This concept is quite popular in the leadership literature and in corporate training programs, motivation and empowerment of employees is what will lead an organization to success. Throughout *Lead Me Out to the Ballgame* we will explore this concept and discuss how this is done with million dollar players, as well as those who 'ride the bench' for most of the season, those players who spend more time watching than playing . When studying major league managers and major league players we see that these players are not very different from employees and managers outside of baseball. As much as baseball is a game, it is also a business which is filled with new hires (rookies), seasoned employees (veterans), and managers who need to do whatever it takes to make them successful. Just as in baseball, when the individuals are successful the team has a greater chance of achieving success, and the organization follows along.

To me the biggest joy for a manager is seeing a player play up to his potential. I mean, not have a great year, they don't have to have a great year, but play up to the potential that you know they have.

Davey Johnson, manager, Washington Nationals

Theory to Practice

The ten *Bases of Leadership* that we identified through our research are all complementary. Just as a center fielder can't play the whole outfield by himself, a single *base* will not work alone to bring about a win. The manager, the coaches, and the team as a whole must work together, just as our winning strategies complement each other to bring about success on and off the field.

As you read through this book we encourage you to think about your own experiences at home, at work, on a baseball diamond, and elsewhere. Think about movies you've seen, books you've read, and places you've traveled. With each of our *bases* think about how often you've seen them used successfully and how often you've witnessed or been a part of them being used unsuccessfully. Our research was fun and exciting to conduct, and we hope that our passion for baseball and leadership comes through loud and clear and helps excite you about leading your teams as well. We hope you will take the time to contemplate your own leadership style, your strengths, the areas you feel you could also use a little coaching on, as well as spend the time working through these areas while you cultivate and develop your *Major League Leadership*. You will find that managing and leading a baseball team is not that different from leading a team of employees you may encounter in your own life. Use the stories, share the stories, and learn from the stories as we bring you into the clubhouses of Major League Baseball!

By the end of this book you will learn some best practices to develop your *Major League Leadership* and apply some of these concepts in your life. As leadership is dynamic, alive, and exciting to discuss we hope that you will share with us some of the ways that you've been able to use our strategies by joining us in discussing leadership and baseball through social media. On our website we have some worksheets, blogs, links, and other resources to help you continue to cultivate and apply the ten *Bases of Leadership* and we hope you will take advantage of this and also join our discussions. We have links to our social media sites on our webpage, www.majorleagueleadership.com, and invite you to head there and share stories with us about how you lead like a Major League manager.

One last note before we throw out the first pitch. One major difference between Major League Baseball and life outside of the Game is that in baseball people change their teams more often than most of us change our jobs. Since we look forward to *Lead Me Out to the Ballgame* remaining on bookshelves for many years, and we don't plan to update this work each season, we've decided to leave the affiliations of the players and managers that we interviewed as the teams that they were associated with at the time of the interview. In other words, as you are reading this book you will probably see players (and managers) associated with teams that are now inaccurate...that's just a part of the game.

So, now that the pregame is over and the anthem has played, let's get to it. It's time for first pitch as we begin to discuss the keys to leading like a Major League Baseball manager and developing your *Major League Leadership*.

Play Ball!!!

Foster Teamwork

Know Your Game

Create a Winning Culture

Communicate Effectively

Cultivate Relationships

Support Your People

Lead by Example

Know Your People

Find Your Passion

Earn Respect

Ten Bases of Major League Leadership

The Ten Bases of Major League Leadership

1. Find Your Passion - Be passionate about your cause and let others see your excitement.

2. Lead by Example - Set the tone for your organization and work with your team to throw the right pitch.

3. Earn Respect - For yourself, for those around you, and for the organization you are a part of. If you want others to follow your lead then you need to show them you can be trusted.

4. Know Your People - Learn the different ways each of your teammates is inspired and under what conditions they work best. Once you know this you can help them to succeed.

5. Cultivate Relationships - Get to know those around you on a deeper level so that they will *want* to work their hardest for you and your organization.

6. Support Your People - Let those around you know that you are loyal to them and will go to bat for them whenever necessary.

7. Communicate Effectively - Be clear with your message and listen closely when spoken to.

8. Know Your Game - Know your business, whatever it is. Become an expert in your domain.

9. Foster Teamwork - Teams which work together are stronger than individuals working alone. Create an environment where people will follow your lead and all exhibit the *bases* we have identified... when you do that the team will work together.

10. Create a Winning Culture - Keep a focus on the short term, day to day goals, but always be mindful of the end goal, winning the season, the big contract, and being a leader in your industry.

Part One

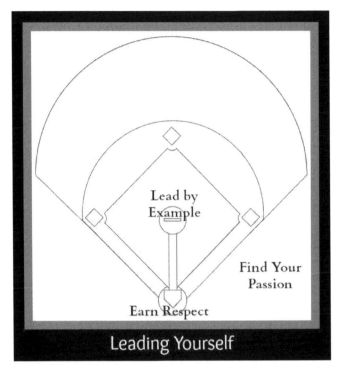

Leading Yourself

Using the baseball diamond as our blueprint, consider the dugout, the pitcher's mound, and the area behind home plate. Together, they form the triangle of inward leadership and the dimension of **Leading Yourself**. Just as the team and the manager begin the game from the dugout, we also begin with our first *Base of Leadership* – **Find Your Passion**. On the mound stands the pitcher who sets the pace for the game and leads the defense with our second *Base of Leadership* – **Lead by Example**. Finally, behind the plate you find the catcher who calls the pitches and encourages the pitcher when needed. To do this successfully, the catcher must have achieved our third *Base of Leadership* – **Earn Respect**.

Before we can lead others effectively we need to first understand how to lead ourselves and present ourselves in a manner that exudes shows confidence to those around us.

- How do you lead in a manner that capitalizes on your strengths and minimizes your weaknesses?

- What are the ways that you can cultivate trust within your team so that they will battle for you and each other every day?

- How do you portray an aura of respect so that your team will respect you and follow you no matter how odd or unique your methods might be?

These are some of the areas of focus for Part One of *Lead Me Out to the Ballgame,* Leading Yourself. Before we can lead others most effectively, and create a strategic game plan, we need to first focus inward and understand our strengths, recognize the impact of our actions, and appreciate the ways which we can present ourselves to garner the respect of those around us.

There's a certain way to play this game. I think that if they [managers] show that, guys gain more respect for them. When they [managers] don't have an agenda... that's really important.

Jed Lowrie, infielder, Houston Astros

In this first part of *Lead Me Out to the Ballgame* we explore the ways that leaders embrace their passion, understand their strengths and weaknesses, model behaviors that they want emulated by those around them, and develop trust with their team so that they can help them to achieve their potential. One of the themes which emerged from our interviews was the need for consistency from managers. Players realize, and managers understand, that in order for people to feel comfortable to make the tough plays and push themselves to extremes they need to know what their manager will do when they are successful, but more importantly what their manager will do if they are not. Players want to know if their job is secure, when they can expect to play, and when they can expect to sit, just as employees in organizations want to know their goals for the day, the week, and the year. Consistency, positivity, and honesty - all themes which were communicated to us as some of the most important qualities for managers to possess, and all themes of leadership which are important for leaders outside of baseball to possess, were some of the specific characteristics that were identified as characteristics of respected leaders. When asked what makes an effective MLB manager and a manager that he wants to play for, Zach Duke's response was that he likes playing for managers who have, "a positive attitude, a willingness to communicate, and honesty." He continued that "letting guys know where they stand, always being an open communicator, and having that open line of communication" are the main components of effective leadership in a Major League clubhouse.

As we will explore through Part One, Leading Yourself, the qualities and behaviors identified as important for leading a major league team are also important in the boardroom, the hospital, the police station, the shop floor, and everywhere else people work and lead, helping others to accomplish their goals. Before we can get on the field with our teams for practice and games we need to head to the batting cages and do some work on ourselves so that we put ourselves in a position to present ourselves best, and lead our people to success.

Chapter 1
Find Your Passion

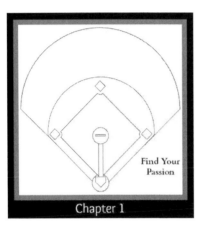

I come to the ballpark with an attitude of here we go, what are we going to accomplish today? I try to keep myself motivated and pumped up when I'm on this baseball field. It's a constant tone; you know how many people sit outside the fences that would love to be doing this job and would love to have an opportunity to be in this uniform? I tell my guys, my players, the coaches, and myself, remember that. It's a special thing and it doesn't last that long. So remember it when you walk out there, enjoy the heck out of this because it won't last forever.

Ron Gardenhire, manager, Minnesota Twins

From the Tin Man in the *Wizard of Oz* to Joe Boyd in *Damn Yankees*, we see that, 'you gotta have heart'! In baseball and in life, the leaders with the most passion are the ones who will be most successful at inspiring their teams. Whether managing a hundred million dollar team like the Yankees or Red Sox, or a small market team with limited capital, it's vital for the manager to project an aura of optimism, passion, and excitement each day. Teams, whether they are expected to win their division or not expected to go very far at all, still need to get on the field 162 times each year and try their hardest, no matter what the odds are against them. Just as in baseball, those organizations that are competing every day for market share must do whatever is necessary to inspire their employees so that they too can win their 'Division[1].'

---

[1] Major League Baseball is comprised of two Leagues, the American League and National League, each consisting of an East, West, and Central Division. Teams compete to win their division in hopes of playing in the playoffs and advancing to the World Series.

Numerous players throughout Major League Baseball identified passion as one of the most important characteristics their managers can have, and our experience in business certainly corroborates this as well. Just as in the boardroom, players want to see their managers excited and they want to see the fire in their eyes. In the boardroom the style managers use to show their passion is different than on the ball field, but the impact is the same. There are many behaviors we can adopt from coaches and managers in sports, and being more visible with our passion and excitement is certainly one of them.

> *When the leader, the guy at the helm, believes and is passionate, it's tough not to feel that same energy.*
>
> **Ryan Doumit, catcher, Minnesota Twins**

OK, let's be truthful here. As much as we try to relate the business world to baseball, for many people the reaction will be the same, baseball is baseball, and work is work. And yes, this is somewhat correct. When we go to work each day we have certain goals we have to meet, tasks we need to accomplish, and people we need to deal with, whether or not we desire to do so. We need to realize though, that even though playing a major league sport is glamorous (and lucrative) some of the same issues still need to be addressed … goals, tasks, conflicts, etc. Just as we face these issues, so do MLB players, and they, like us, need their manager, their leader, to guide them to winning ways.

Now that we've broken the myth that baseball isn't *all* fun and games, that there is work that needs to be done each day, we can now tell you that it is still playing baseball, and baseball is definitely fun! This is something that was expressed to us by managers, players, executives, and members of the press. Those who we interviewed appreciate that each day that they are blessed to be in the position they are in, but also realize and acknowledge the work, the pressure, and the stress that goes into it each day. Regardless of how bad a day might be, no matter how many runs your team may be down, or how stressed you may be about having to deal with the press after a game, you are still standing in front of thousands of people and working in the game you have loved since you first hit a ball off of a tee. Mike Scioscia, manager of the Los Angeles Angels of Anaheim explained in a 2012 interview for MLB.com that, "even the worst days that you have on this job, it's still baseball … you're doing something you love. It's a privilege to be able to do something you have such a deep passion for. I don't take that for granted." It's this attitude that drives Scioscia as well as the other managers and players we met to work hard each day, and it is an appreciation like this that will drive all of us to excel at our jobs and in our lives.

As players and managers noted, it isn't hard to get excited and passionate about a sport they love. But what about in business and our everyday work lives – can we be passionate there too? The short answer is absolutely! Motivational speaker, Tony Robbins tells us to "Live with Passion!", and he ensures that he does this every day of his life. In 2011 the world lost an iconic leader, Steve Jobs, but we will continue learning from him for years to come. Jobs gave us many lessons, to keep things simple, to continue to innovate, to have confidence, to surround ourselves with the best people, to collaborate, not to be afraid to be different, and to share our vision. The one thing that is a common thread through all he did, passion! Steve Jobs truly loved what he did and let his passion and enthusiasm shine through to the world. This is one of the secrets to success, we need to focus on what we love and find ways to capitalize on it.

Compassion and Hope

Having a positive attitude is one of the important ways to demonstrate our passion to those around us. Toronto Blue Jays pitcher Darren Oliver, as well as many others throughout the league, told us that they consider being positive to be an important managerial skill regardless of the game situation or time of the season. It is no surprise that over the course of a full season players will slump, just as it is no surprise that over the course of a year, employees will fall into ruts. What is important for managers in all walks of life to remember is that when guys are struggling, that's the time they need their manager to stay positive, be compassionate, and help to pick them up. The importance of celebrating small wins is evident here. How easy is it to do this when you have 162+ games per year, numerous at bats per game as a hitter, and batters to potentially strike out as a pitcher. If we only look at the single outcome, only look at the overall goal of winning the World Series, we will lose track of the small wins that keep us going each day.

Kansas City Royals Manager, Ned Yost, talked to us about his own positivity, and how his positive attitude is apparent because he has so much fun watching his team perform. He talked about the fun he has when he gets to watch his team play, and the joy he gets from seeing them perform successfully. His whole day, he told us, is built around them; as a leader, it is all about his team. This is an important concept, and one which is important in all walks of life. As former president Ronald Reagan said, "The greatest leader is not necessarily the one who does the greatest things. He is the one that gets people to do the greatest things."[1] Helping your people achieve at their highest level certainly helps you be successful as well. To do this most effectively, you must truly believe in your people and find joy in their success.

I'm proud of these kids every single day when they come in and they work hard and they play hard. I don't care if they've gone four for four, I don't care if they've gone 0 for four. It's the way they go about their business and their mindset, and what we're all trying to accomplish together.

Ned Yost, manager, Kansas City Royals

Let's step out of baseball for a moment and talk about one of Barron's 30 best CEOs in 2012, Howard Schultz, chairman and CEO of Starbucks, and the man who will forever be known as bringing the words Grande and Venti to our vocabulary. Schultz is a man who is known to lead from the heart and as someone who leads based on his values[2]. As a teen, Schultz was impacted deeply when his father's employer showed no compassion and fired him after being injured on the job. Schultz uses what he learned and felt from this experience and applies it by providing health benefits to part-time workers and demonstrating compassion in his decision-making. Providing healthcare is important to attracting and retaining talent and Schultz's determination to stand firm increased employee commitment and loyalty. His heart said to take care of his people, and he did. Not every gesture we make with our team needs to be grand like Howard Schultz providing healthcare, there are other ways a manager, a leader, can show you that you are important and that they believe in you and the organization that are easier for many of us to do. Bringing in Starbucks (or Dunkin Donuts) to your team just 'because', giving employees an opportunity to 'dress down' on a Friday in September because it has been a long quarter, etc. These are not big expenses, but they are actions that will have a great impact on those around you. It's important to remember that no matter what level you are in, you can show your passion by showing others that you care.

A positive attitude naturally brings feelings of hope, and hope can influence the behavior of others in a very positive way. Hope helps people to not only see the future but also to see themselves achieving it and being successful. Hope is energizing, engaging, contagious, and increases our spirit and ability to be resilient. Some important keys to successful leadership are understanding the right time to praise, the right time to coach, and the right time to sit at the end of the dugout and contemplate your next big play. By leading with heart and compassion, we can provide the hope that others need to keep striving for their goals.

Enthusiasm and Energy

Major League Baseball is unique in that there are a minimum of 190 games between spring training and the regular season. On top of that, if a team makes the playoffs, another 20 more games can potentially (and hopefully) be added to that total. That's over 200 baseball games, and as much as you love the game, it can certainly get tiring! Oakland A's manager, Bob Melvin, explained to us that getting a team energized for so many games can be quite challenging. An average day for a baseball player is a lot more than playing a game for three hours a day as some spectators believe. Players and staff arrive at the ballpark approximately seven hours prior to game time, spending that time strategizing, conditioning, and mentally preparing for their daily competition. Again, baseball is fun, and they are fortunate to be a part of it, but let's not forget that it is still a job, nearly seven days per week, twelve hours per day, with late nights, early morning travel, and for up to ten months each year. Different from what many casual baseball fans think, baseball is not just a few hours a day of playing ball!

The manager's job, according to Melvin, is to prepare his players physically and psychologically for the long days and night. For these reasons, Melvin explained, sometimes he needs to 'wake the team up', sometimes scream a bit, and more often by giving them a little extra encouragement. As with most of our jobs, some time each day is spent doing things we enjoy, but much time is also spent doing some things that we do not. It is up to the manager, the player, and the coaches, or in the world outside of baseball, the managers, employees, and team members, to keep a focus each day on the goals they are trying to achieve. Melvin also discussed with us how he tends to push his players harder when they are winning than when they are losing because he knows that when the team is not performing his players are already down and not in the mindset to fully appreciate his message. This message was reiterated by another great manager, Joe Maddon of the Tampa Bay Rays; we need to know the right time and place to address important issues. The goal is to generate energy and enthusiasm, to influence each player to be the best they can be every single day, and thus when a player has a bad game, either not producing the way he is expected to produce, or making an error that costs the team a game, this is the time to support him and offer compassion.

Melvin recounted for us an instance during the home stretch of the 2012 baseball season when his Oakland A's were in the hunt for the American League West title. During a game in September when the A's were playing the New York Yankees in the Bronx, Melvin's team had a bit of a setback. They had been up by four runs in extra innings and ended up losing the game. There were three errors made in the game, but none more troubling to first baseman Brandon Moss than when his fielding error allowed the winning run to score with the bases loaded and two outs in the 14th inning. This is the type of situation when a manager must get mad and rant and rave … right? Imagine, you are winning in extra innings, imagine you have been working overtime for weeks to finish a key project, imagine you are close to winning a bid on a major contract. Now imagine your first baseman, your project manager, your proofreader, makes a mistake and the game, project, bid, is lost … angry doesn't begin to describe your feelings. Let's imagine now that your project manager had completed many projects for the organization already during the year, or your editor had caught and fixed many errors in previous works that secured grants for your organization. Let's now think about Brandon Moss who had a terrific 2012 and helped his team to eventually win the American League West title. After the game Brandon Moss was expectedly upset, feeling quite bad about the error. Melvin's response was to approach Moss and remind him that over the course of the season that he had singlehandedly won many games for the A's. Moss appreciated this comment, and let Melvin know that Melvin's approach and comments were very meaningful to him.

Leadership is not about what you accomplish, it is about what you get others to accomplish. It is about influence, empowerment, realization of potential, and the reach of your impact. These definitions all revolve around the concept of influence and around the energy that one has. There is no better way to influence others than by allowing them to see the passion you exude for a cause, a project, an organization, or a team. In most cases this passion is exhibited with a positive action, but in some, as is the case when managers are at a heightened state of arousal (for example, when an umpire errs on a call), passion can be displayed a bit differently. Let's consider for example, Sweet Lou, former major league baseball manager, Lou Piniella, who would get the fans up on their feet cheering and yelling, when he managed. Lou showed his energy to his team through exuberant actions which got them excited and helped them to push forward in their games. When Lou was upset with a call he would kick dirt and sometimes lift and throw bases across the field. Piniella influenced anyone who would see or hear him through the passion he displayed. Energy = Influence, in baseball as well as in life.

Lou Piniella communicated energy by kicking dirt; others communicate it through their tone of voice. Toronto Blue Jays infielder, Omar Vizquel, who at age 45 was playing in his last Major League season when we met with him, has plenty of experience playing for different managers and coaches in his career. His veteran observation was that players engage more when they have a manager that is loud and has a firm voice. He explained that a manager's intensity really opens a player's eyes and helps players to realize the significance of what they are doing on the field. When a manager is intense, positive, and gets excited, then players will feed off that and get excited as well. Vizquel's point to us that a manager needs to be loud isn't something that all players and managers agreed with, in fact, many managers pride themselves on the fact that they are calm and collected. Great managers lead differently based on the situation they are in and the people they are leading...something we will discuss further in Chapter 4, the importance of knowing your people.

A great example of this comes from our time with Joe Maddon in the manager's office of the Rays spring training complex, and specifically what happened at the end of our interview with him. Maddon is someone who takes great pride in his demeanor. He is an intellectual, someone who is truly a 'thinking' manager. That said, as with all managers, sometimes the rationality we possess and take pride in can be overcome in the heat of the moment. At the conclusion of our interview with Joe we asked for a picture to be taken with him. Joe positioned the picture to be taken in front of a photo which he had hanging on his wall. The picture was of Maddon, the intellect, bellowing at an umpire. Energy and passion … it comes out in many ways.

Energy is often expressed through intensity, a characteristic that is embodied by many Major League Managers. Brad Ziegler, Arizona Diamondbacks pitcher, discussed how the way his manager, Kirk Gibson, communicates his intensity to his players affects them on the field. Gibson expects his players to play hard for the entire game, regardless of the score. Ziegler said that Gibson has helped him to understand that maintaining intensity can affect outcomes; if not today, perhaps tomorrow. One of the ways that another successful manager, Ron Washington of the Texas Rangers, demonstrates his intensity and energy is through dancing in the dugout as his players run the bases, appearing as excited as a little leaguer whose team has just taken the lead on their cross town rival. He doesn't do this all the time, but next time you watch a Rangers game peek into the dugout if possible when something exciting happens on the field. Interestingly, we have learned that Washington's dancing when his players get a hit has made his pitchers a bit jealous if he doesn't dance as much when they pitch. Washington cheers, runs, jumps, and high fives his players and coaches; not only feeling his excitement for the game, but showing it and thus empowering his players to do the same. Exciting, intense, passionate … these are some of the ways Washington has been described, and the impact this has on his players is tremendous. By showing his passion, Washington engages his team to be passionate as well. His players want to win because they want the 'Washington Shuffle' to be put on for them. So whether you are a quiet leader or you like to raise your voice or dance around to generate energy, know that your level of enthusiasm and energy is contagious and your team will take cues from you to understand the norms of successful behavior.

Optimism and Happiness

Staying positive and optimistic is important for both managers and players in Major League Baseball just as it is important for leaders and followers in the 'real world'. The old axiom, a bad apple spoils the bunch is accurate, and similarly, a bad attitude can and will spoil a team. Maintaining a positive attitude not only affects the outcome of a baseball game but also work performance, when workers are happy and engaged in their work, they will perform better. Happiness at work is not something that is difficult or expensive for managers to foster, but it is something that takes energy and a commitment to a team environment.

Having a positive focus is a perspective that has gained quite a bit of attention in the areas of psychology, leadership, and business over the past decade. The idea that we should focus on the strengths we have and build on those as opposed to focusing on our weaknesses is something many leaders have realized. In baseball, as Diamondbacks pitcher Craig Breslow told us, players often watch videos of themselves striking out or not making great contact with the baseball as opposed to watching videos of when they are most successful. This focus is one that transcends the business world as well. Managers often spend time evaluating what an employee is doing wrong as opposed to pointing out to them what they are doing right. It is a positive leadership focus that Breslow points to as useful for a player's success. He noted that too many managers focus on fixing what is wrong versus learning to prolong what is going well. He provided a great example of the latter with his former Oakland A's manager, Bob Geren, and how he would comment when he was pitching really well: "He [Geren] would call me in and say, 'I just want to let you know, you're pitching great, we need you out there.' I think that, probably more so than talking about why things are going wrong, [being positive] keeps guys succeeding."

Baseball is a game of failure, so there's a ton of negatives you can focus on. When somebody's always pushing you toward the positive, always making a positive out of something, that helps a lot.

Scott Moore, infielder, Houston Astros

Joe Maddon made a point of sharing that his style and his attitude hadn't changed in his years of managing. When his teams were young, inexperienced, and losing, he maintained the same style and attitude as today, managing a more experienced and winning team. One of the ways that positivity can be used as a motivator is by focusing on what a player is doing right as opposed to focusing on what they are doing wrong. Baseball is a game of small wins, getting a hit one out of every three times will often earn a player a spot in the Hall of Fame. Staying positive when you are leading or playing on a winning team is easier than staying positive when a team is losing. Staying positive in an organization that owns the market is easy; however, staying positive in an organization where uncertainty surrounds you is much more difficult. How do we do this? The first step is attitude, and more importantly, consistency within one's attitude, as Joe Maddon told us, "I walk in the door and am the same person everyday regardless, win or lose, good or bad".

The degree of impact a manager has is only as significant as the players he can actually put on the field, and one of the most important things a manager can do for his players is to help them to "stay upbeat," and not allow losses to "crush them," this according to Cleveland Indians manager, Manny Acta. We see that positivity is an important trait to feel but an even more important trait to convey to a team … even in tough times; the manager must appear to be in control and portray a positive attitude. It's up to the managers as well as coaches to portray a sense of optimism each day to their players … if they don't do this then the players will not perform to their potential.

Manager Ron Gardenhire of the Minnesota Twins explained how important it was for him to stay positive and optimistic regardless of what is going on. He discussed how if he is in a bad mood, that will transfer to his players and even his coaches. Gardenhire wants everyone to understand that they are going to accomplish something today. Gardenhire stresses that there are many people who would like his job, or that of his coaches, or his players. He realizes that it is a special honor to be a part of Major League Baseball and that it won't last forever … so he reminds everyone to be happy and make the most of every day.

I come to the ballpark with an attitude of here we go, what are we going to accomplish today? I try to keep myself motivated and pumped up when I'm on this baseball field.

Ron Gardenhire, manager, Minnesota Twins

Bob Melvin shared an example of a manager who he worked under and learned from, and the way that this manager portrayed a positive example to his players and coaches. Melvin learned from Bob Brenly when he was in Arizona with the Diamondbacks organization. Even though Brenly was a first year manager, they won the World Series that year. However, Melvin learned the most from him when they were losing – he learned to always stand tall, keep your head up, and be in the forefront for your team. Melvin stated that, "I think that's very important because if the manager's sitting back on the bench with his head down or pissed off, that's how your team's going to react. I really remember noticing and watching Bob when we were behind, that he never sat down in those times, he never went back into the dugout and sat back on the bench; he always stood tall on the top step and showed his team that we were there for 27 outs."

Standing tall on the top step and showing the team that you are there not only for them, but with them. Standing on the top step of the dugout vs. standing 'in' the dugout; standing in front of a podium when addressing an organization vs. standing behind the podium; sitting amongst your employees vs. sitting in front of your employees. As minor league pitcher Zach Miner shared with us while with the Kansas City Royals in spring training, "if he's positive, he comes to the field every day, ready to strap it on and get a win, I think players will fall in line and take to his lead". You get the idea, staying positive, being with your people, and showing them that you believe in them ... all leadership behaviors that make employees happy, and in turn, lead them to greater levels of performance.

Keeping it Real

With a positive attitude and inspirational hope also comes a caution. We need to be careful that our passion and excitement remain in check...it can be a short jump from high fiving and dancing in the dugout ala Ron Washington to a tirade such as those displayed by Lou Piniella, Ozzie Guillen, and others. There are times when a positive attitude and all smiles approach may not be appropriate; instead the team (or player) may need a dose of reality. When Bob Melvin was brought in to manage the last place Oakland A's in June of 2011, over a third of the way into the baseball season, he was faced with a team that was nine games under the .500 mark, laden with injuries, and certainly not very positive and optimistic.

Bob Melvin brought with him the experience of managing two previous ball clubs, and a reputation of being a 'player's manager'. It was up to Melvin to show his passion and motivate his team, but also be realistic with them that the chances of them winning their division were slim. One of his former players, pitcher Craig Breslow, said about Melvin's arrival to the A's that it was important for Melvin to excite his players about their different individual goals, goals that in turn would lead to the overall team goal, playing hard and winning games. Breslow believed that Melvin did a great job motivating them. He went so far as to tell them that they would not be making the post season but that didn't mean they didn't have goals or something concrete to achieve, for example, a job or free agent contract. Breslow stressed that it is important for managers to be honest and direct so that players understand that they may not be returning to "this" team next year but they were playing for millions of dollars. It was Melvin's passion and optimism for the game that led to a renewed energy in 2011 and helped him to receive a three year contract after the season. It is also his passion as well as the ability he has to empower his players that has led his 2012 team of formerly unproven players to be a post season threat. Today's managers need to keep their people optimistic about winning, and more importantly about how their individual successes will lead to the successes of the team. It's important for managers to navigate outside pressures and entities and protect their teams as much as possible from these pressures. Players see the roster and scoreboards just like the fans and realize that they may not be the 'team to beat', but even so, they need to keep pushing ahead and focusing on the possibility of the win.

Becoming a Passionate Leader

It was great listening to Major League Baseball managers talk about how they love to have fun with their teams, and even more fun contemplating how we can take these lessons and use them to help those of us outside the baseball world to lead like a major league manager. Team building activities and humor have long been used as methods to strengthen connectivity and raise morale in the workplace. We know from research and practice that humor can strengthen team solidarity and help bring about creative and innovative problem solving. In fact, many effective leaders use humor to achieve objectives, create teamwork, and generate creativity.

It may seem that passion, having a positive attitude, and encouraging fun is an odd grouping of leadership behaviors; however, when you pull it all together, what we really have here is an authentic approach to leadership. Authentic leaders utilize hope, positive emotions, identification, trust, and optimism to influence the behaviors and attitudes of their followers. These types of leaders lead with their heart, and everyone around them knows what they stand for. They are the real deal; they don't need to be someone else. These leaders inspire, bring people together, and motivate everyone to create value. Leaders who are authentic pursue their purpose with passion, live their values, lead with their hearts, cultivate relationships, and demonstrate self-discipline. These are all behaviors which show your people who you are and show them that you are focused on them as well. By demonstrating our passion, our compassion, our positivity, and our authentic self, we are leading ourselves in a way that others will be engaged by our actions, want to follow us, and hopefully want to lead themselves and those in their lives in this manner as well. Now that we've discussed the first *Base of Leadership*, demonstrating passion, we will now move on to the second, garnering respect from our people and showing it to them as well.

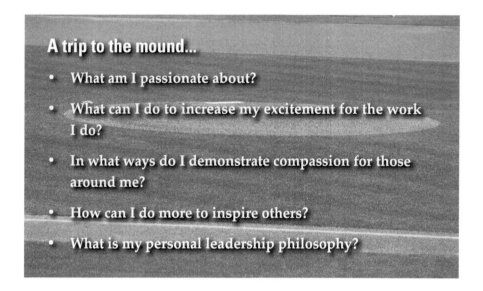

A trip to the mound...

- What am I passionate about?

- What can I do to increase my excitement for the work I do?

- In what ways do I demonstrate compassion for those around me?

- How can I do more to inspire others?

- What is my personal leadership philosophy?

Chapter 2
Lead by Example

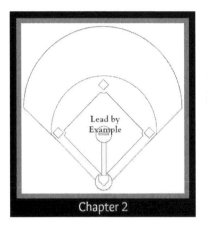

If you want to be a leader, the first person you have to lead is yourself.

Mike Scioscia, manager, Los Angeles
Angels of Anaheim

As a leader, all eyes are on you. People look to you to see how you react in situations, what you do when you think no one is watching. Your actions establish the norms and culture of the organization and that is one of the many reasons that leadership carries with it such a great responsibility.

One story of leading by example has been told many times – it is about Mahatma Ghandi in the 1930s. Legend has it that a mother stood in line for hours to speak with Ghandi because her son was addicted to sugar and she hoped he could convince her son to change his eating habits. When she finally got the opportunity to make the request, Ghandi requested that she return in two weeks and he would speak to her son then. She didn't understand the reason she was being sent away; nevertheless, she did as Ghandi instructed. Indeed, two weeks later she returned with her son and Ghandi immediately spoke with the boy and told him that he should not eat sugar. The boy agreed to start on the journey of improving his diet. The mother thanked Ghandi for his compassion and wisdom but then had to know why he asked her to return in two weeks instead of speaking to her son right away. Ghandi replied, "Upon your visit two weeks ago, I too was eating sugar." He further explained that until he had taken the journey of giving up sugar, he could not teach the boy to do it. Ghandi understood that to be authentic, you must lead by example.

Kouzes & Posner, the authors of *The Leadership Challenge*[3], refer to this as modeling the way. A leader's behaviors must reflect what they say and what they ask others to do. Likewise, the remarkable Coach John Wooden believed that our personal example was paramount. Wooden wrote, "I believe there is no more powerful leadership tool than your own personal example. In almost every way the team ultimately becomes a reflection of their leader"[4]. Similarly, when we asked Eric Hosmer, first baseman of the Kansas City Royals, what he believed were the qualities of a good leader he noted leading by example; a leader, he said is, "someone who has to be true to their word and someone who has to lead by example. If he's the leader of the clubhouse, if someone kind of sees him going in the wrong direction, that's who we look up to, and that's who we feed off of. So he just has to be someone who sets the example and carries himself the right way."

Leading by example - How you carry yourself around the clubhouse, how you go about your business, how you go out there and train, how you perform. Without saying much, it's just doing it.

Gio Gonzalez, pitcher, Washington Nationals

In this chapter, we explore what it takes to lead by example and share stories from Major League Baseball and the business world that demonstrate both good and poor examples of this. We explore the role of our values in our leadership and look at how self-control builds our credibility as a leader, as well as how emotions can sometimes be detrimental to what we are trying to accomplish. Leadership is often about teaching so we examine ways that we teach through our behaviors. Finally, we discuss ways that you can effectively lead by example.

Values Establish the Baseline

We hear a lot of talk about values, but what does that really mean? In a basic sense, values reflect how an individual distinguishes right from wrong. They are things that are important to us and something we find intrinsically desirable. Values are typically viewed as being positive and greatly contribute to the moral and ethical attributes of our character. In considering the impact of values on our actions we often ask, what is most important to you, and what are your values? To be authentic, we must ensure that our behaviors reflect our values, as behavior is the foundation of leading by example. As we move forward in this chapter, consider, do your behaviors reflect what you value most, and do your behaviors represent this?

Great leaders have a commitment to a set of values and they are passionate about what they believe in. Such leaders operate on principle and we know it when we see it. Did you ever know a leader who was constantly changing his or her position? That is likely because they weren't truly clear about what they believed in – they were not grounded in core beliefs. Values provide us with a moral compass to navigate our lives. You must know what you care about in order to lead authentically.

We can find this type of values-based, authentic leadership in successful organizations. Howard Schultz (Starbucks) and Jim Sinegal (Costco) each state that employees are valued and demonstrate this by providing healthcare insurance at a low cost to their employees. Both of these organizations have satisfied employees which results in high quality service for customers as well as a low turnover rate with high performing associates. John Mackey (Whole Foods Market) and Ronald Shaich (Panera Bread) believe in quality foods and have thus designed their organizations with that value as paramount. Mackey is the co-founder of the conscious capitalism movement which is centered on making a primary purpose of business the improvement of our lives and the creation of value for stakeholders. Shaich, living out the mission of "A loaf of bread in every arm," ensures that all leftover baked goods are given away each night. He also established Panera Cares Cafes that allow customers to pay what they can afford as opposed to setting prices for items as is traditionally the norm. In 2013 Panera launched a campaign called "Live Consciously. Eat Deliciously" which aims to raise awareness about hunger in the United States, another indication of the strong values that they espouse. Schultz, Sinegal, Mackey, and Shaich are passionate about their values and have found ways within their respective industries and organizations to transfer them to their business practices each day.

Baseball is really no different than any other organization when it comes to the impact of values. Executives, managers, and players all have certain core values which drive their actions both on and off the field. These values provide a guidepost by which other interactions and decisions are made, these values are the foundation of all that transpires. During our interviews, conversations, and observations, several values surfaced within Major League Baseball. They included the following:

Accountability	Diligence	Hope	Preparedness
Collaboration	Fun	Integrity	Sacrifice
Commitment	Growth	Inspiration	Service
Determination	Hard Work	Passion	Teamwork
Development	Honesty	Perseverance	Winning

John Farrell, manager of the Toronto Blue Jays, told us that when they search for players they consciously look for people who will reflect the values of the team. For them, it is important that they not sacrifice what they value simply to get a win, it is just as important that they play the game the right way and can be proud of their actions. It is important to Farrell that all of his actions are true to his and the organization's values. This comes through in his personal behaviors and with his interactions with coaches and team members. For example, if he were to suddenly advise or even hint to a player that using performance enhancing drugs (PEDs) might help them recover more quickly or maybe get more power from his swing, that would be completely against his values and the team's values because Major League Baseball has banned such substances. Doing so would send a confusing message to all who work with him. Farrell (and other managers) understands that he must maintain an authentic message regarding not only their personal values but also the team's espoused values.

We have certain values that we uphold from a personal character standpoint to a team professionalism approach ... this is what the Toronto Blue Jays stand for. This is what we value, both in terms of the type of people we have, the way we play the game. Ultimately, we want to win the right way.

John Farrell, manager, Toronto Blue Jays

Values based leadership is a leadership philosophy which focuses on the ability to connect personal values to an organization's mission and goals. When the values of the manager are congruent with those of their team, commitment and motivation of all involved will be increased. Authentic, values-based leaders are able to demonstrate their beliefs by acting upon their personal values and beliefs while ensuring that their behaviors are a reflection of who they are as people. These behaviors are the epitome of leading by example; with a focus on values we are truly walking the talk. As Clint Hurdle, manager of the Pittsburgh Pirates, shared with us, "it's nice to be able to speak well, get together, and share your thoughts; but actions match up so much better over time." Hurdle explained that if he expects his players to have a positive attitude whether or not they won the game the day before, he needs to have that attitude he, "... needs to walk in like that every day."

When we appeal to values, we are truly appealing to the heart, helping us to connect with people on a deeper level because we are reaching the core of their belief system. Being able to accomplish this can be inspiring because we are connecting with what gives them meaning and causes them to take action. People want to be authentic to their values as it can fill them with pride and make their work feel worthwhile, and those around them want to see this authenticity. As Jarrod Saltalamacchia, catcher on the Red Sox told us about his former manager Terry Francona, "he always came to you, cared about what you were going through and how you felt". The authenticity exhibited by Francona showed Saltalamacchia and the rest of his team that Francona was authentic and truly cared about the well being of his players. When a manager is authentic and shows his care for his players, this rubs off on the players, and, as Hunter Pence, San Francisco Giants outfielder explained to us, they are apt to exhibit this compassion as well. Pence said, "At the end of the day, it's about being there for each other. It's about sacrifice. It's not about yourself. So, you're getting there. Part of that, I guess in the long run, being a good teammate is being prepared to help your team win. And that's the work ethic, that's the mindset, and getting your mind, your body, and everything ready to go."

This same sense of pride in your leader can be very powerful and managers through the game want to see that authenticity in their players just as managers throughout industry want to see this in their employees. When a connection is made at a deep level and it is understood that you each desire very similar things in life then the relationship can develop and performance in turn will increase. When you pull it all together, it seems to come down to pride. People want to be proud to lead their team; they want their team to be proud to have them as a leader; they want everyone to be proud of the organization. In baseball, this includes an entire community of people. As Ned Yost, manager of the Kansas City Royals said, "Play the game in a fashion that will make our Kansas City Royal fans proud." We all want to be proud of where we work.

> *When you go back to leadership, when you have pride in leadership and you believe in your leader, you come to work with a smile on your face, and have pride in playing for this organization.*
>
> **Bob Melvin, manager, Oakland A's**

Hold on to your Helmet

Part of leading by example includes exhibiting self-control. Coach John Wooden wrote, "Self-control creates consistency – a hallmark of great leadership. It starts at the top with you, the leader, and must be taught by word and deed to your entire team."[5] By *word and deed* – again, leading by example – allowing our actions and behaviors to reflect what we believe in and deem to be important. In the workplace, employees like to know what to expect from their manager. They desire a leader that is patient and understanding; one who sets a good example by walking the talk. The same was found to be true in Major League Baseball. Josh Donaldson, Oakland A's, discussed with us how he finds patience to be one of the best assets a manager can have.

Donaldson said, "I think patience is probably the biggest thing - that even-keel kind - I think that's what helps me the most."

In baseball this is very true as well. Ned Yost, manager of the Kansas City Royals, stated that, "I think you have to have patience, one" in response to what he believed to be the most important qualities of a manager. Interesting that he noted patience and not another of the many qualities typically associated with leadership; perhaps because he understands that when we are not patient, it may be difficult to exhibit other important qualities. Similarly, Josh Donaldson of the Oakland A's, talked about how he finds an even-keeled temperament to be very important in a manager. He said, "Things are going to go wrong now and then, so for them to be patient I think is one of the best assets they can have." As things do go wrong in baseball, in the workplace, and in our personal lives it is important to understand how to best present ourselves in times of turmoil, as in many cases this is what defines us to others.

Unfortunately, when we do not handle situations with grace and understanding – when we lose self-control – this can often become more defining of our leadership and of who we are than all the appropriate things we do on a daily basis. Think of baseball tantrums that you have witnessed either in person, on TV, or perhaps from just watching a YouTube video. Lou Piniella, Charlie Manuel, and Earl Weaver are just a few of the MLB Managers who are known for their on-field tantrums, both with 'outsiders' like umpires as well as with their own players. Let's not forget the epic melt-down of Braves AA Manager, Phil Wellman on June 1, 2007 which has generated nearly 750k views as of this writing! Wellman's nearly 30 years in baseball has been over-shadowed by one singular incident. In our own lives we are faced with many 'bad calls' just as our counterparts are on the baseball field. When an employee finishes a project and it is not correct or a vendor delivers a subpar product, it is up to us as to how we react, and thus in our control how we are remembered. We don't want our legacy to be one of losing self-control.

Many view patience as a virtue but really what patience is centered on is exhibiting discipline. What makes patience so important? It seems that the world is moving at break-neck speeds and faster is typically viewed as better. In broad terms, learning to be patient can help you in three ways: in your relationships with people, in your decision making, and in your health. Leadership involves people and people require patience because as we know, we are imperfect beings. Patience allows you to take the time to understand people and help them develop at their preferred rate of speed, which may be different from yours. Patience provides the opportunity to listen, and through listening, you gain greater understanding. We have probably all experienced the overly demanding or argumentative manager or co-worker. When we encounter such an individual, we tend to stop listening and simply let their tirade become background noise. But when someone approaches us with patience and understanding, we want to listen and engage in conversation.

In baseball and in industry one of the key tasks as a manager is decision making... we depend on our leaders to make decisions, and we depend on our leaders to make the right decisions. During time of stress the great leaders stay calm and clear-headed, they maintain composure and come to battle prepared. Leaders who desire to reach long-term strategic goals need to demonstrate patience and self-control versus merely reacting to a particular situation or throwing a tantrum. Manny Acta made a point of telling us that he believes it's important to maintain control on the field to send the right message to his players, "it's okay to stay under control...you don't have to be kicking dirt and throwing stuff and yelling and screaming." So why is it that managers often, as discussed above, react in heated fashion on the field? Well, the reason quite often is that their passion, as discussed in Chapter One, takes over, and this is why it is so important to always be considering how your actions are interpreted by those around you. It is patience which can assist in thoughtful decision-making as it helps you to resist those impulse reactions which can lead to rash decisions.

The health and well-being of leaders is another area where leaders must be careful; they must look after their health because being a leader is demanding both mentally and physically. Leadership can be stressful, and impatience leads to stress and triggers anger. In their book, *Into the Storm*[6], Dennis Perkins and Jillian Murphy chronicled how a tiny vessel, the AFR Midnight Rambler, physically one of the less impressive of the boats in a 628 nautical mile annual race in 1998. In this race, the Sydney to Hobart race, in 1998, the AFR Midnight Rambler achieved unexpected victory under treacherous conditions, their amateur crew competing against much more experienced sailors and much more impressive ships. One of the lessons identified from this adventure is the need for the captain, the leader, to rest so that he can always be ready to take the helm at full capacity when he was rested. Leaders sometimes need reminding that they cannot go full throttle all the time, that having them at full force when they are there is more important than having them tired and performing at less than their full ability . This is an important concept as it is important for all of our team to be rested and ready to go when needed, and if the leader doesn't follow his or her own advice it is harder for them to encourage it in others. Andrew Bailey, Boston Red Sox relief pitcher shared with us that players often don't want to take a day to rest and the good managers know when to encourage it as they know they are more likely to succeed when physically and mentally rested.

Joe Maddon discussed how in today's culture yelling as a form of discipline or perceived motivation doesn't work. We see this in both theory and in industry as the way employees respond best is not by empowering and not by bullying. Maddon empowers his players (as discussed throughout this work) by fostering a team approach. As many players shared with us, they know when they have made a mistake or made an error on the field, and they also know what they *should have done,* so it isn't necessary them to be told by their manager. Maddon encourages positive discourse amongst his team by demonstrating it himself. Players told us that they reached the level they did in their 'business' for a reason, and it's important and empowering to them when their manager acknowledges them for that and also continues to help them grow. Players know, as Mike Trout, All-Star outfielder on the Los Angeles Angels of Anaheim, told us about successful Major League managers, "they're always trying to lead you in the right way. They won't lead you in a wrong way. They're trying to teach you new things each and every day."

When discussing people who had influenced his style of leadership with the San Diego Padres, Skipper Bud Black noted Dick Howser. Howser was the World Series championship team manager when Black pitched for him with the Kansas City Royals, and he said that what he gleaned from Howser's leadership was, "his patience, his loyalty to players, his belief in his guys, in certain players; not being a roller coaster of emotions with his players on performance." Self-control is really about managing emotions which requires an understanding of emotional intelligence.

Developing Emotional Intelligence

As we've addressed, at the heart of leading yourself is a strong understanding of who you are, how you may react in situations, and how you can control your emotions and actions. These precepts correspond to Daniel Goleman's concept of emotional intelligence[7]. Goleman identified four attributes: self-awareness, self-management, social awareness, and relationship management, as keys for successful interactions. The first two include how we understand and control ourselves and how such awareness is important in effectively leading by example and walking the talk. To be most effective you must understand how your emotions work and how they affect your behaviors. It is important that you have self-confidence and know your weaknesses as well as your strengths. Managing yourself by controlling impulses and emotions, being adaptable, and demonstrating commitment are key components of leading by example, as Gio Gonzalez, pitcher on the Washington Nationals shared, "it's better to be seen than heard." This concept is fitting for managers, players, and all of us, you must lead yourself before you can lead others. How can you read the emotions in others if you cannot first read your own?

Brandon Guyer, of the Tampa Bay Rays, was one of many players we encountered who noted that preparation was important for managers and that managers need to keep an even keel to have the greatest impact on their players. Guyer said, "Not getting too high, not getting too low when the team's down, maybe have a meeting or something, just give us a little talk. You know a lot of leaders, I think lead by example, just by the way they prepare. Just the way they do their work. I think that makes a great leader." Guyer's manager, Joe Maddon, also brought up the topic of emotion when discussing how players sometimes do not look their best with the media due to a lack of control. Maddon said, "You can control your response and keep the emotion out of it. I think a lot of times where the athlete looks bad publicly through the media, he chooses the wrong response – he chooses the wrong way to go with the whole thing. And sometimes, it is emotion based; sometimes it is ego based where you start going in the wrong direction."

How you behave as a leader establishes the boundaries for what is acceptable for your team. A volatile leader causes people to focus more on how to avoid making their boss mad than they do on their work. Actions become focused on avoiding negative consequences versus creating a winning organization. Manny Acta talked about how the public often has contradictory expectations for the way Major League Baseball managers and players should act. He shared, "When you're doing good, and you're cool and you can keep your emotions in check, it looks nice; but as soon as you're losing, people think that you're too laid back." He went on to say, "It's okay to stay under control. It is very blown out of proportion to think you have to be kicking dirt and throwing stuff and yelling and screaming in order to make people believe you care." Matt Joyce of the Tampa Bay Rays talked about his manager, Joe Maddon, with a lot of admiration. He attributed his calm and even tempered leadership as a reason Maddon has won Manager of the Year honors more than once. "He never panics, he never flips out, he never yells or screams, it's always a constant personality and reaction that you're gonna get from Joe, and you kind of know what to expect."

We are fortunate to have many emotionally intelligent CEOs today. One leader we discussed earlier, for example, Howard Schultz of Starbucks. Schulz left the top leadership role at Starbucks for several years but came back because he truly cares about this company and the people that work there. He appreciates people at a deeper level and states openly that he functions out of love. Schulz is passionate about building a company that that his father never got to work for in his years of struggling in a blue-collar job with no health insurance. Another well-known leader, Warren Buffett, is extremely loyal to his team and empowers (and expects) his CEOs to run their companies as their own. Buffet must be doing something right because the CEOs stay with the Berkshire family, they do not go to competitors, and most also avoid retirement. In the world of mergers and acquisitions, this is almost unheard of. Ursula Burns, the first African-American woman named as the CEO of a major American company, leads Xerox by being extremely direct and assertive but her values-based, mission-centric approach inspires those around her. Burns was raised in the Lower East Side of New York, in a difficult neighborhood, by a single mother. She started with Xerox in 1980 as an intern and steadily worked her way to the top position. Through all her success, she has maintained humility by being self-aware and authentic. These are all examples of emotionally intelligent and self-aware leaders who are very successful. These leaders are people who value their employees and do what is necessary to develop relationships with them by understanding their needs.

Emotionally intelligent leaders are often easy to recognize as it is easy to be around them. They are typically very open and don't get defensive but instead, listen and engage in conversation to reach a higher level of understanding. Such leaders are highly empathetic and seem to know the right way to deliver a message even when the news may be unfavorable. Leaders with high levels of emotional intelligence are "available" on both a physical and emotional level for their team members; just as John Farrell, Davey Johnson, Joe Maddon, and other successful managers who make a point of spending time getting to know their players so that they can connect with them on a personal level. When conflicts do arise, these leaders can use their skills to quickly diffuse the situation and guide it to an effective resolution. This is all possible because they do not operate on ego and they remain vigilantly aware of their own emotions while providing an empathetic focus on others.

Teaching through Behavior

At the crux of leading by example is the fact that what leaders do – their behavior – is continuously teaching others. People view our behavior and place more credence in what we do more than in what we say. This may include being on time, demonstrating respect toward others, our general work ethic, and exercising self-control. Our desire should be to allow our behavior to be a wonderful teacher to not only our team members but to all around us. Coach John Wooden stated, "Your own personal example is one of the most powerful leadership tools you possess. Put it to good use: Be what you want your team to become."[8] Angels' manager, Mike Scioscia, lives this philosophy as well. Scioscia shared in an interview, "If you carry yourself the way you should, if you carry yourself the way you should as a person, then the players are going to respond to that. I think if you look at the guys who've been successful, Major League managers, who've been in successful environments, I think they set the environment at first in how they carry themselves."

Bob Melvin learned this a long time ago and keeps it at the forefront of his mind each day, "As a manager you have to be careful about your outlook every day when you come to the ballpark. I've learned over the years that there's going to be some difficult losses, some are more difficult than others. How you carry yourself the next day has a lot to do with how your team comes out and performs. They really take the lead from you, your coaches, and the manager, and how you handle those types of situations. They need someone that stands tall and exudes that type of leadership." What Melvin is describing here is a form of teaching – he is teaching his team through his personal behavior.

In any position of leadership, I think for me, I refer to being able to be a teacher ... the ability to lead, to have people take your message and follow and motivate. Those are the three things I look for in my position. I want to be a teacher, a leader, a motivator of my group.
Bud Black, manager, San Diego Padres

Great leaders are also great teachers. They challenge us in many ways and through those challenges, we learn to experiment, take risks, learn from our mistakes, and experience the satisfaction of discovery. Leaders who teach don't simply tell us to "go figure it out." Instead, they prepare us, share their experiences and insights, and inspire us to be inquisitive and knowledge-seeking. Leaders who are teachers will let us fail because they understand that it will help us to learn.

However, they will also encourage us while teaching us that we must be accountable to ourselves. Although they may likely let us fail, they will not let it be a fatal fall!

Sometimes you may hear a manager say, "But I don't want to be a role model, I'm just a regular guy trying to do my job." Is it possible to be in a leadership role and not be a role model? The answer is no. If you are in a position of authority and people can see your actions and behaviors then you are a role model. Leaders are mimicked; people will model themselves after their leader's actions and try to emulate them. If you are modeling and teaching behaviors through your actions, then it is important that you create a teaching and effective modeling environment. This can be accomplished by taking the initiative to truly teach and coach others to assist in their development.

Mike Scioscia learned about being a good role model from his mother. She stressed to him that it wasn't just important to be a good baseball player or a coach or management, but to be a good person. The Angels manager went on to say, "We're all role models, not just because we're in baseball; kids are role models when they are seven years old and don't realize it because there's somebody that's five that's looking at what they do. I think the qualities of a Major League Baseball manager are really the same in anything, in any walk of life. I've found that to be true."

How You Can Lead By Example

Leading by example is an important part of self-leadership. To be successful, you must understand your core values, exhibit self-control, practice emotional intelligence, and remember that you are always teaching through your behaviors. People will follow your lead whether that is positive or negative. You can call upon your values in many situations. Use your values when you have passion for a topic as they will allow you to speak authentically. Appealing to values can be extremely effective when what you desire is commitment more than compliance. In times of crisis appealing to values can help you provide hope and get the team focused.

I think everyone kind of follows the lead of their manager. If he's positive, if he comes to the field every day ready to strap it on and get a win, I think players will fall in line and take to his lead. If the guy's real negative and always kind of down on guys, I think that's when you get teams that get split and have clubhouse problems.

Zach Miner, pitcher, Kansas City Royals

Leading by example and modeling behaviors is constant; thus, we must recognize this and use it to our advantage versus allowing it to become a hindrance. As we become cognizant of our actions as well as our words; people will model what they see us doing. Leading by example comes back to being authentic – being yourself – and exhibiting who you are every day. Bud Black, of the Padres, offered some great advice on this topic, "First of all, a person's got to be himself. That's number one. You can't be something that you're not. So whoever you are as a person, you have to be that person, you can't be somebody else. You can't try to emulate other leaders or other people in leadership positions because people will see right through that. So I think the main thing is to be yourself when it comes to leadership. That's number one."

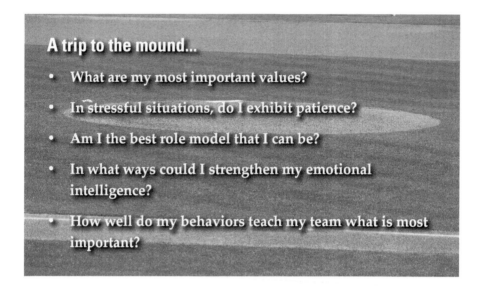

A trip to the mound...

- What are my most important values?
- In stressful situations, do I exhibit patience?
- Am I the best role model that I can be?
- In what ways could I strengthen my emotional intelligence?
- How well do my behaviors teach my team what is most important?

Chapter 3
Earn Respect

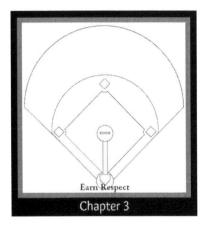

I don't care how long you've been in this game or what kind of success you've had in this game; every day you have to gain their trust, and every day you have to gain their respect.

Davey Johnson, manager of the Washington Nationals

Respect … it's hard to hear or read that word without a vision of Aretha Franklin belting it out, it is something that we all seem to crave and sometimes wonder if we will ever earn enough of it. As Aretha said, we need to 'find out what it means to me', and to us, even more significant, is finding out what it means to the organization or team as a whole.

- How does a manager having the respect of his players impact their commitment and play?

- How does a player having the respect of his manager impact the team?

- How does respecting your organization impact the work that you do?

Rodney Dangerfield spent his career proclaiming, "I get no respect," and as you read through this chapter think about the respect you get, the respect you give, and the impact it has on the players in your life.

There is a basic notion when discussing leadership that people follow those who have power. This concept however needs a little explanation in that power does not and should not come from a person's position alone, but should come from who they are and what they do. The power should come from the person, not the position. It's true, as Ned Yost, manager of the Kansas City Royals pointed out, "when you become a manager, right off the bat you garner respect because you're a manager." This is the positional power we mentioned above, and a power that many people throughout the world rely upon. This type of power however, only goes so far. As Yost continues, "you've got to earn that [respect] every single day." We may get a person's respect from our position initially, but we will either keep it or lose it depending on our actions once we are there. Following a leader or a manager solely because they are in charge will take us far enough to avoid getting reprimanded or far enough to do a *good* job. Following someone because we respect them and what they stand for will bring us to levels of performance that will lead to greater personal and in turn greater organizational success.

For me, having played under 8 or 10 managers in the big leagues already, I think the managers that are more successful and get the most out of their players are the ones that just expect you to be professional, show up on time, play hard, and at the same time, let you be the player you have to be in order to make that happen. Treat you like a human being and treat you with respect, that's pretty much it.

Jose Bautista, infielder, Toronto Blue Jays

In baseball the actions that players or managers take become public discourse, are often amplified by the media, and can have impact much greater than one win or loss. Terry Francona's departure from the Red Sox after the 2011 season was well documented with him, according to many, losing control of the team and losing the respect of some key players. In September of 2011, with the Red Sox still fighting for the wild card, Francona was disrespected publically by one of his pitchers, John Lackey, when he headed to the mound to make a pitching change. When Francona made the decision to remove Lackey from the game he had given up 11hits, 2 walks, and 8 earned runs while pitching $4\frac{1}{3}$[2] innings...not a good outing. Most of us can understand that at that point, it is time for the pitcher to turn the ball over to the bullpen and try to stop some of the bleeding. As Francona walked to the mound the dismay was clearly visible in the eyes of his starting pitcher. Lackey glared at his manager, licked his lips, and waited. After the game, Francona, as he often did, praised his player for his efforts as opposed to condemning him for his ineffectiveness. Although it is necessary as we will discuss in Chapter 6, for managers to support their players, players must support their managers as well, showing them respect on and off the field.

Respect the Manager

We often hear the axiom that actions speak louder than words, and this is certainly the case in Major League clubhouses. Like his colleagues throughout the league, Bob Melvin, has had to deal with some bad apples in his career, most of us have. One of the things which successful managers realize is that when dealing with issues pertaining to players or employees in any type of organization it is important to act swiftly and act appropriately so as to send a message to the team that certain behaviors will not be tolerated. Complications sometimes occur when information is spread throughout a group that doesn't accurately depict the situation that occurred, and this is something managers at all levels should try to avoid. Managers

---

[2] Barring 'extra innings' coming as a result of a tie score, a baseball game is comprised of 9 innings.

need to communicate with their teams about the situation and how it is being handled so that they continue to have confidence in their manager that negative situations are dealt with appropriately.

Bob Melvin shared with us that in the past he had some players on his team who had a difficult time buying into the team philosophy. Players, as he identified, that were more consumed with their numbers, their contracts, and their own accomplishments, than with the team and organizational goals. In one instance, Melvin explained, he had a player who was spreading information throughout the clubhouse that was untrue, causing problems for himself as well as the team as a whole. He shared how he called the player into his office to discuss a situation and they had "a little run-in." When telling his teammates about the meeting with his manager, the player's story differed from what actually occurred. According to the player, he stormed into the manager's office and "did things that didn't happen." This was a situation where a player did not demonstrate respect for his manager, his team, or his organization. The outcome, the player was released. Cutting ties with this player sent a message to the team that the front office stood behind their manager, supporting him in his handling of the situation, and standing behind him to his team. The player did not show respect, and, in Melvin's words, "was the wrong guy for the situation." He was not a fit for the Oakland A's.

What's important to point out in regards to respecting the manager (or for that matter, respecting the players, the team, or the game in general) is that the first step in cultivating a culture of respect is putting together a team comprised of people with not only the ability to hit a ball, make a play, or throw strikes, but a team of people with a moral compass. In order to cultivate a culture of respect the team should be constructed of people with drive and character, a team comprised of people who *want* to be a part of it, and a team of people who will do what is necessary to support the team as a whole. Talent is important, but fit is vital. We as leaders need to, as Jim Collins, author of *Good to Great* points out, "start by getting the right people on the bus, the wrong people off the bus, and the right people in the right seats."[9]

Getting the right people on the bus is something that Bobby Cox, the now retired iconic manager of the Atlanta Braves, played a large role in doing. He not only focused on the development of his players, but in the selecting of players for his team that would be a good fit for the culture of the Braves. Cox was known for picking a certain type of player for his team, the type of player that would add to his team's chemistry, not detract from it. He chose players who did not have discipline problems, didn't complain to the media, and didn't try to bring attention to themselves. From these criteria you can see why Bobby Cox's managerial legacy includes four Manager of the Year honors, and why he holds fourth place in managerial wins in Major League Baseball.

Cultivating the respect of the players as a Major League manager must do is not any different than earning the respect of an employee or a colleague in any organization, so how does one do this? To borrow a line from the Smith Barney commercials with John Houseman from the 1980s, "he earns it!" Sean Burroughs, who we spoke to when he was a member of the Minnesota Twins, pointed to honesty and openness as two of the things which lead him to respecting his managers. A manager needs to be honest with his players about their position on the team, what is expected to them, and what they need to do to succeed. They need to be "true to their word, and true to what they preach". As infielder Eric Hosner of the Kansas City Royals told us, "the players notice that, and then [they] gain a lot more respect."

Bud Harrelson, though only a manager for a short time in the major leagues, is a baseball 'lifer', and has been a player or coach since the 1960s. We met with Harrelson in Long Island, NY, where he is part owner and coach of the Long Island Ducks, and from the first few moments with him realized that he was a natural teacher and loved the coaching aspect of the game. Bud earns his respect from his players by his actions. He spends time with them, teaches them, and when necessary, lets them know how things should be. One story he shared with us dates back to his time as manager of the New York Mets in 1990. On the 1990 Mets, there were some very strong personalities including Darryl Strawberry, Doc Gooden, and the person who we will discuss now, Gregg Jeffries. In 1990 Gregg Jeffries was in his second full major league season and was still learning the appropriate way to deal with his frustration. Harrelson told us that quite often Jeffries would throw his helmet and gloves on the ground by first base when he reached there and found out he was out. After a little while Harrelson made it clear to his third baseman that the first base coach is not his "caddy", he is a major league baseball coach, and should be treated with respect. Harrelson told Jeffries that he would be fined $100 for his helmet and $100 for his gloves each time he did that in the future. Soon after, Bud had a check for $200 in his hands. Harrelson, being the 'buddy' and coach to everyone, decided to hold on to that check for a while, and when the team traveled to California, Gregg Jeffries' home state, Harrelson returned the un-cashed check to him, thanked him for changing his behavior, and told him to take his parents to dinner. Bud established his respect through his actions and at the same time managed to change the behavior of his player to show respect for the Game.

Honesty

The impact that an honest manager has on a player's development is far reaching, as retired catcher Eddie Taubensee told us. Players both young and old discussed the impact of open communication with us. This will be explored in a later chapter in detail, but one of the key components to successful communication is honesty. In our interview with Eddie Taubensee we learned how he was lucky enough to have Davey Johnson as his manager early in his career on the Cincinnati Reds as an eager and passionate young player. Johnson was honest with Taubensee and let him know what his role on the team would be and what he needed to work on as a player. It was the honesty, Taubensee told us, that led to his great respect for his manager. Taubensee admitted that he didn't like the answers he got, but he respected his manager for being up front with him. Today, years later, Taubensee appreciates the message that he was given and the work he did because of it. From our interviews with some of Johnson's current players on the Washington Nationals it seems that his style hasn't changed much, he is still as straight forward and honest as ever. One of his veteran utility players, Mark DeRosa, told us that honesty is the "biggest thing that motivates [him]", saying, "at least I know where I stand."

As much as anything, I try to be honest with them and let them know what's going on.

Don Mattingly, manager, Los Angeles Dodgers

Stories detailing the importance of honesty were heard throughout our interviews both inside and outside of baseball, and honesty (within limits) was pointed to as a way to earn the respect of players. When a manager doesn't have this, and a player, according to veteran Jose Bautista, cannot trust the information that is being presented, this can make for an uncomfortable situation, one that Bautista hopes doesn't impact many players. This concept is one which transcends the world of baseball and is quite simple when we think about it; if you don't trust the intentions of another person, for how long will you follow them? If you don't trust their intentions and believe them to be honest, the rest aren't quite as important.

Don Mattingly, as well as Royals manager Ned Yost, echoed similar views on trust, it isn't something that you go out and intentionally try to earn, but it is something that develops over time. Learning the best ways to develop and sustain trust is something that all of us need to do as we develop our leadership toolkit, no matter what industry we are in, and no matter what position we are in. One way to cultivate trust within an organization is by being upfront about intentions as much as we can. Certainly there are instances where information does not, and should not be shared, but if we have established a relationship built on trust and respect with our team, they will understand that we have our reasons for keeping some information private.

I think for me honesty is the biggest thing to motivate me...you might not always like what you hear, but it's the truth. [With it] you can walk away feeling good about where you're at at a certain point in your career, and make the necessary adjustments to change people's minds.

Mark DeRosa, outfielder, Washington Nationals.

In the Dodger's clubhouse respect for the manager is an outcome of Don Mattingly's genuine concern and care for his players, "I want them all to be great; I want them all to have the best seasons they can possibly have, so I always have their best interests at heart." When this is known and communicated in a straightforward and honest way, then respect and trust will develop. Ron Washington, manager of the Texas Rangers, is also one who we spoke with and is known for his straightforward approach. It is well known by his players that if he tells you something, you can believe it. Kyle Weiland, pitcher, Houston Astros, discussed what he wants to hear from a manager, "I think the most important thing is to be straightforward with guys. Tell them what they need to hear. If it's bad stuff you've got to take it and try to turn it into your strengths...that's what you want to hear, the things you need to improve on."

When we asked Michael Taylor, an outfielder in the Oakland A's organization, what he thought was an important leadership characteristic, he summed up the feelings of players very appropriately when he said that players want honesty. "They don't want managers to sugarcoat situations. Honesty will allow a guy to kind of sit back, assess the situation, make a decision for himself and his career. Honesty, definitely." As much as people appreciate honesty, we realize that sometimes this can be difficult to give. Ned Yost, for example, pointed out how he as a manager certainly doesn't want to hurt his players' feelings, but also does not want to lie to them or misrepresent anything.

Trust, Equity, Consistency, and Persistence

Trust can be defined as the feeling that one person has that the intentions of another are for the best interest of the whole, not for their own personal best interests. It is a confidence in the intent and actions of another. As was discussed in the opening of this chapter, without trust, a relationship can only go so far, and a player or employee will only do so much. Matt Sinatro has been around the game of baseball for over thirty years as a player, coach, and executive. In his time he has worked with some of the great baseball managers and players and has learned quite a bit about building relationships and cultivating trust with them all, to him it is the key to success for a manager as well as a coach in baseball. Something that Sinatro said to us that is important for leaders in all walks of life to understand is that trust and agreement are two very different things, players and managers are not going to agree with everything, but in the end, if you gain their trust, the players will go along with the decisions you make.

Let me tell you about trust, you have to get this trust factor going early in your career. It's more important that they [your players] have trust in you, than what you say. You might be the best coach, but if they don't trust you, they're going to always be concerned what to do. You may not be a very good coach with x's and o's, but if they trust you, they'll do anything you say; they'll run through a wall for you. You have to get trust early. The longer it takes, the tougher it is to get.

Matt Sinatro, coach, Houston Astros

So, how is trust developed? The simple answer is that it comes from relationships, the building of relationships, and the cultivating of relationships each day. Ron Roenicke, manager of the Milwaukee Brewers, explained that to him, the building of trust is not having a focus of winning at all costs, as mentioned by some players, but it's showing his players through actions that not only does he care about winning, but he cares about them as people, he cares about their careers, he cares about their families, and in general, he cares about their well being. In 2011, when a horrific earthquake and tsunami hit Japan, Takashi Saito was not thinking about baseball, but thinking about his family who were in the middle of the devastation. His manager, and the Brewers organization as a whole, made it very clear to Saito that baseball is not the priority now, and he didn't need to be at the ballpark. Roenicke's direction to his bullpen ace, do whatever you need to do to take care of your family as well as yourself.

Another way that trust is developed is by players knowing that their managers 'have their back', that they support them unconditionally. Red Sox pitcher Craig Breslow shared that to him, the way a manager can earn his players' trust is by standing up for his players to "anyone and everyone that questions them, whether that's the boss, whether that's the GM, the owner, an umpire, or another team," the manager should have your back. Breslow's sentiments about this were echoed by players throughout baseball as well as by many managers we spoke with, and supporting their players is a *Base of Leadership* we will discuss in Chapter 6.

On the trust part, my job is to make them understand that I have their back, good or bad.
Ron Washington, manager, Texas Rangers

Ron Washington became quite passionate when discussing with us the relationships that he builds with his players. To him, it is important that his message is always consistent and that it is delivered for as long as it needs to be. In other words, until it is received! Washington, like many who are passionate about their beliefs, does whatever necessary to communicate with his people. He knows his game, he knows how to be successful, he has confidence in his abilities, and, according to him, "I'm gonna keep preaching what I know is the right thing... I will never stop saying, or preaching the message."

As you have seen, treating players fairly is an overarching theme in this chapter as this is one of the ways a manager can cultivate respect and thus motivate his team. Years ago an interview aired on WFAN New York where Jim Leyland, manager of the Detroit Tigers, was asked how he has been so successful over his many years as a manager. Leyland's response was quite poignant, he responded that he 'treats everyone the same, but everyone differently.' In this response Leyland hit on a key means of earning the respect of players or employees; they each need to be treated differently, but they each need to be treated equitably. Equitable treatment creates significant outcomes for managers as when people are treated fairly they will in turn respond with greater loyalty and commitment and the manager's credibility will rise leading to a more attentive and focused player.

This is something that no matter what industry we are a part of that we can and should be aware of.

Respect through Experience and Credibility

If you have experience and credibility on or off the field, according to some players like Will Rhymes of the Rays and Lyle Overbay of the Diamondbacks, you will gain the respect of your players. Players, as any of us should do, evaluate from whom a message is coming from prior to determining the value of the message. As we've discussed, managers have credibility simply because of the position they are in, but they also need to keep it through their actions. When someone who had great success on the field such as Kirk Gibson becomes a major league manager, he brings with him a level of credibility and respect, right off the bat. Gibson's fire and drive as a player, personified by his limping around the bases after hitting a game winning pinch hit homerun in Game One of the 1988 World Series, gives him instant respect. What it gives him in addition to this respect, however, is the power to tell his players, I know what it's like to be hurt, and I know what it's like to have to sit the bench in a key game, and I know what it's like to win. Gibson had fire as a player, and has fire as a manager, both of which continue to earn him respect from his team. Overbay, points to Gibson's 'track record' as the way his trust was earned initially, but then points to his honesty and leadership as the way his trust and respect are cultivated.

When you become a manager, right off the bat, you garner respect because you're a manager, but you've got to continue to earn that every single day.

Ned Yost, manager, Kansas City Royals

Veteran infielder Jamey Carroll talked with us about how some of his former managers earned his respect. He pointed to the ability of his managers to be able to develop relationships with their players, be their friend, but also be able to push them and hold them accountable when necessary. It is a balancing act that managers in and out of baseball deal with, and one, when perfected, can lead to success. As Carroll said, when a manager has to reprimand a player and the player *doesn't* react with a statement like, "wow, I thought we were friends yet you're yelling at me", then the manager has built a level of trust with that player. He talked with us about his time playing for Frank Robinson when he managed the Washington Nationals. Carroll respected Robinson; not just for his success as a manager and a player, but for the way he dealt with his players. The respect Carroll has for Robinson was mutual, as Robinson was quoted as saying that "every team needs a Jamey Carroll"[10] because of his work ethic, his drive to do whatever it takes to make himself and his team successful, and his positive attitude no matter what his role was that day.

They know that we played, and that's all fine and dandy, but that can only go so far, they get tired of hearing the old stories of stuff. If you're phony and all you're doing is telling stories but not working, they see right through that.

Alan Trammell, coach, Arizona Diamondbacks

Gerry Hunsicker, Vice President of the Tampa Bay Rays, noted how complex the game is today due to free agency and the money that players can command. This environment, he told us, means that managers cannot lead through intimidation or pure discipline like they did in the past. Instead, "he [the manager] has to have the respect and be able to keep the interest of the players." Terry Ryan, longtime general manager of the Minnesota Twins, echoed some of the thoughts of Hunsicker when we discussed respect with him. To Ryan, it is vital that the manager gain the respect of his clubhouse, "if he doesn't, you're in trouble!" Although during our interview Ryan identified the significance of respect as a key leadership trait for MLB managers, he too was identified by his players as being someone who should be respected. Colorado Rockies pitcher Jeff Manship, who spent parts of four seasons with Minnesota when we spoke with him in 2012 identified Terry Ryan as a 'perfect example' of someone who tells people how things are, without sugar coating them, "he tells you how it is straight up", Manship said, "and I think guys appreciate that. They don't want you saying one thing when they really mean another."

Respect through expertise and credibility comes from a manager's reputation but also through their actions on a day to day basis. How a manager acts under key situations will lead to whether or not a player has faith and respect in his decisions. Managers like Joe Maddon who "lead with their gut" need to have success in their past decisions in order for players to believe in the ones they make today. Ron Washington is one who has had success as a manager in his career, and as the current manager of the Texas Rangers, brings with him a winning record into the 2013 season. Even with his success, the zealous Rangers manager often gets second guessed for his self-proclaimed management by instinct. This second guessing, however, comes more often from the media and the outer circle, than from his players and coaches who have learned to trust and respect their manager and his actions. The managers who are successful in the major leagues, just as those who are successful in industry, have earned their respect through their actions. In order for mistakes to be accepted occasionally it is first important that credibility in the field is established...in baseball that means getting some wins!

You show them respect, they show you respect. Whenever the guy tells you something, you might not know if it's right or wrong, but you know that he's got your best interest at heart. So it's a lot easier to follow.

Louis Coleman, pitcher, Kansas City Royals

As we've explained, the more positive outcomes a manager can achieve with his team, the more credibility he will garner. John Farrell told us that to him, credibility is key, "you've got to have a credible message, you've got to be consistent, and there's got to be an awareness." In other words, the manager needs to be aware of all that is going on, and be able to communicate a consistent message to his team. This sentiment was echoed by Willie Bloomquist, infielder, Arizona Diamondbacks, "Whether playing bad or playing good. Make sure you're consistent. Consistently positive, moreso than consistently being an ass. That's the biggest thing. You treat everybody the same. No matter what the situation is, be professional and treat everyone respectfully and consistently."

Respect the Team

It should go without saying that in order for a person to perform to their potential they should have a respect for the organization they are a part of. In our travels throughout Major League Baseball we heard a recurring phrase from the managers we spoke to, a phrase which was used by Kurt Russell portraying Coach Herb Brooks in the 2004 movie *Miracle* about the 1980 U.S. Olympic hockey team which won the Gold Medal, *the name on the front* is *more* important than the one on the back! It is up to the leadership of the organization to create a culture where the *name on the front* is representative of pride and generates respect from those who wear the jersey. How a player should appropriately show respect for the team differs from one manager to another. It may be through attending community events which many teams encourage their players to do, or it may be through dress code when players are traveling from one city to the next. Bud Harrelson, for example, told us how when he managed the 1990 Mets, a team with rising stars but also a team with very strong personalities, he needed to teach the team about showing respect for not only themselves, but for the game. One of the things that Harrelson did was to implement a formal dress code during travel days. He shared that at first many players fought back but after a while they began to understand the image that a group of well dressed players portrayed as they walked through an airport or arrived at a visiting ballpark. He also shared that the players began to take this to an extreme and it became a competition between them as to who could wear the nicest clothes!

If you compete to beat the other club, you are respecting the game of baseball. If you respect the person, your teammate and the game, you're gonna compete, you're gonna play hard, and you're gonna have a lot of energy.

Brad Mills, manager, Houston Astros

Creating respect for a team or an organization is obviously not something that can be done by changing a behavior alone, it but must be done by changing attitudes. Bud Harrelson worked on changing the attitude of his players by being forthright with his rationale for altering the dress code, and cited examples of his former managers and peers and the respect they garnered. Building respect is about creating a culture where there is a focus on trust and accountability at all levels.

They gain my respect and my trust by how they perform.

Davey Johnson, manager, Washington Nationals

How does one earn the respect of his peers? His supervisors? His team? These are questions to start pondering and that lead us to our next questions, what can an organization do to encourage and cultivate respect, not only for its people, but for the organization or the team itself? We talked about honesty, transparency, credibility, and other dimensions which lead to a person earning the respect of another, and now we will discuss another way that people earn respect, through doing 'good'.

The great management and leadership guru Peter Drucker proclaimed that "Management is doing things right; leadership is doing the right things."[11] This statement demonstrates the differences between management and leadership, and also demonstrates that both functions are vital to the success of any team or organization. When we consider leaders like Bill Gates, who are greatly respected for their work within their industry and outside of it, we can understand how respect can be garnered. Bill Gates should be respected for the work that he has done for computing, his innovation and business acumen which have made Microsoft a leader in its field. Bill Gates, however, should be even more respected for the good work that he has done with the money he made from his business success through his foundation, the Bill and Melinda Gates Foundation. He, as many other leaders, went from doing things right to doing the right things, and this is something which will bring a person the respect of those inside and outside of his or her inner circle. We all don't have the resources of the Bill and Melinda Gates Foundation, which at the end of 2011 had distributed over $25 billion dollars to those in need; but we all do have the ability to donate our time and resources to 'do the right thing'. This, along with our actions on and off our 'field' will lead to those around us respecting us, and in many cases, as we will discuss in a future chapter, emulating our actions.

[A manager] has to care about his players, that way they will follow. He has to show character. He has to be honest, whatever it takes, and treat everyone like a man.

Bruce Chen, pitcher, Kansas City Royals

It is appropriate at this time to mention that many of the players and managers who participated in our research for this book lead their own nonprofit organizations which raise money for causes which are important to them. The website *The Good in Sports*[12], is a resource to learn about these charities, and we hope that you will visit it and find a cause close to your heart. To that note, portions of the proceeds of this book will be donated to the Strike 3 Foundation, a charitable organization which raises money for pediatric cancer research, and is led by its founder, Craig Breslow - "I started the Strike 3 Foundation to help ensure that every child is afforded the opportunity to prosper."

As we've been discussing, it is important for players to have a respect for their manager and their team, but let's not forget that leadership is about teamwork and that for a team to be most successful, the respect needs to go both ways. Earning the respect of a manager in baseball is not very different from earning the respect of your manager outside of the game, you need to come to work on time (early is even better), give 150%, show *them* respect, be authentic in your words and actions, and go above and beyond in all you do. If you do those things, then more often than not, your manager will put the effort in to help you develop and reach your potential.

If you go out there, work hard, give 100% every time, and show him respect, I think in turn he'll have respect for you.

Phil Dumatrait, pitcher, Minnesota Twins

There's a lighthearted phrase which is often shared, *All I really need to know I learned in Kindergarten.* The concept is that the main lessons in life that we need to be successful are taught in kindergarten, and if we master those then we can be successful in all that we do. Some of the things we learn in kindergarten include sharing, playing fair, keeping our hands to ourselves, and basically respecting ourselves and others (there are more such as flushing, washing hands, and others that are also important, just not as relevant here). These concepts make sense, and these concepts can most certainly lead us to be valuable members of our teams, no matter what those teams are.

Having respect for the manager, having a manager who respects his or her people, having respect for the organization you work for, and having a respect for what you as an individual are doing, these ingredients together are what will bring out the best from the individual and in turn from the organization as a whole. A culture of respect will lead to success on and off the field, in and out of the workplace, and with all those who see the individual and who he or she represents.

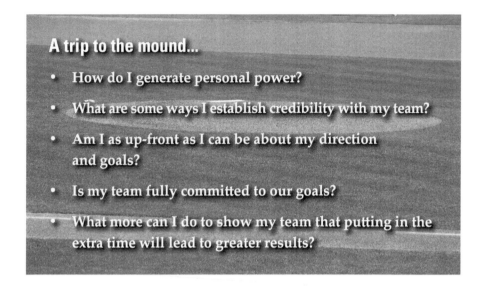

A trip to the mound...

- How do I generate personal power?

- What are some ways I establish credibility with my team?

- Am I as up-front as I can be about my direction and goals?

- Is my team fully committed to our goals?

- What more can I do to show my team that putting in the extra time will lead to greater results?

Part Two

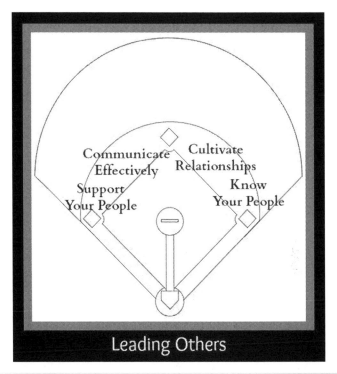

Leading Others

Continuing with the baseball diamond as our blueprint, the focus here is on the infield. Think of what a tight-knit group the infield is, and the relationships that they must develop to work well together. People and relationships are the most important considerations for *Leading Others*. Just as the first baseman must know the base runner and watch that he doesn't attempt a steal, leaders need to understand their team members through the next *Base of Leadership – Know Your People*. The second base position is shared by the second baseman and the shortstop, and this requires working as one, and understanding the importance of the next *Base – Cultivate Relationships*. The third base position is the 'hot corner' in baseball because screaming line drives tend to head that way. The person fielding this position must make the play to support the team like the next *Base – Support Your People*. Finally, the shortstop position covers second, may back-up third, and is often part of a double-play. All of this requires the skills of the next *Base, they must Communicate Effectively*.

Passion, leading by example, and earning respect. The first three chapters of *Lead Me Out to the Ballgame* focus on finding our passion and designing ways to explore and capitalize on it. Part One explored the importance of modeling the behaviors that we want those around us to emulate so that they, as well as the team, can benefit, develop, and excel by doing so. The importance of presenting ourselves in a positive manner and creating situations where our players, whoever they are, can see us as authentic leaders was also explored. By viewing managers as people who have their team's best interest at heart, trust and respect for actions and managerial direction can be established. We spent the first part of *Lead Me out to the Ballgame* working and studying ourselves so that we can put our best foot forward to those who are around us and so that we can begin our next set of *Bases of Leadership* with a focus on leading others. In Part Two we will focus outward and explore the ways that we get to know our people, develop relationships, support our players, and build camaraderie and cohesion on a team through authentic and engaging communication.

During the course of the season I try to find time to say hello, look every man in the eye, and try to find time during the day to have some honest conversation.
Clint Hurdle, manager, Pittsburgh Pirates

As Clint Hurdle, manager of the Pittsburgh Pirates, as well as most of the managers we spoke with, shared with us, *Cultivating Relationships* with our team is one of the keys to successful implementation of our plan. So, how do relationships get formed? Well, let's think about our own lives and our own relationships both personally and professionally. We form relationships by getting to know the other person; and once we do, we decide if we want to pursue a relationship, and if so, what type. In business, in baseball, or in our personal life, in order to be most successful with those around us we need to know what they are driven by, know what they are interested in, and know what will motivate them to move in a path that will be beneficial for themselves, for us, and for the common goal.

Current hitting coach and former All-Star infielder Howard Johnson told us that one of the things that most managers have going for them is that they are "not so far removed from the players and their experience that they don't know what it's like." It's important for managers both inside and outside the Game to understand that each person is different and needs to be understood in order for the manager to work with them best. Diamondbacks coach and former manager of the Detroit Tigers, Alan Trammell, said that he learned an important lesson when he played for the Tigers. "We had a great manager in Sparky Anderson", Trammell told us, he [Anderson] would say, "you like to treat everybody the same, but that's really not the case. You have to deal with each individual differently." In Chapter 4 we will explore this *base* in great depth, in order to be successful it is important to **Know Your People**.

Once the personalities, drivers, and goals of each individual player are understood it is then time to focus on the individual needs the players have. One of the *Bases of Leadership* which came up in our interviews was that players have a deep appreciation for and need for the support of their managers. Players want to know, as All-Star Bryce Harper told us, that no matter what, they want their coaches to be there for them and let them know, "hey, we got your back."

When a manager sticks up for his team, when a manager shows us he's a part of the team, and not part of the front office or something like that, I think that's a big thing, we're all here together, front office included. But there's a lot of stuff the players go through as a team that the manager sees, so it's nice to have him on board.

**Jarrod Saltalamacchia, catcher,
Boston Red Sox**

Our final *Base of Leadership* in Part Two, and one which works in conjunction with all the *bases* throughout this book, is how to **Communicate Effectively**. The study of leadership is not difficult to understand, but can sometimes, depending on our own strengths and abilities, be difficult to execute. The key to success in many of the situations in our lives is our ability to communicate our ideas and our vision to those around us. As we close out *Leading Others* we will explore the ways that our managers communicate with their teams, help their players set and achieve goals, and work with their coaches to help their players to reach and even surpass their expectations.

Chapter 4
Know your People

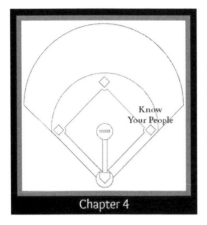

Chapter 4

Some guys need loving on, and some guys need you to get in their rear end a little bit...I think more [to be a successful manager], you have to be a good manager of people.

Josh Willingham, outfielder for the Minnesota Twins

Imagine walking into a new job as a manager and not looking around at the people you will be managing and not thinking about the specific situation the department is in. Imagine walking in and just managing as you have done in the past. Well, this seems a bit silly (and dangerous!), and rationally we all know that *we* wouldn't do this, so why, in many cases does it occur? According to some leadership scholars we all have a certain style of leadership that we follow, some of us are primarily focused on getting the job done, others are focused mostly on our people and helping them to work together, and others are focused on the situation, and reacting to it. Each of these styles has its pros and cons, and each can be successful at some times and a failure at others. The key thing to know before even attempting to decide what style of leadership we should use primarily in a given situation is that to be successful we must first take the time to get to know the people that we intend to lead.

> *It's very important to be consistent every day, to be positive. There's a lot of failure in the game of baseball, and just recognizing that, and just figuring out ways to make each player better every day which is different for every player [that's what's important].*
> **Todd Helton, infielder, Colorado Rockies**

The above isn't rocket science, it makes perfect sense. In order to inspire our teams we need to understand what it is that engages them, what it is that drives them, and what it is that makes them *want* to work their hardest for us and the organization. We want them to work their hardest each and every day because they have a desire to do so, not because they *have* to do it to receive a reward or to avoid a punishment. Those people who work just to keep their job will work just hard enough to keep it; those people who work because they want to achieve success for themselves or because they have a respect and appreciation for their manager or organization will go above and beyond. According to Davey Johnson, one of the ways to inspire his people to go above and beyond for themselves and their team is to manage each of them differently. Based on his over 30 years of managerial experience Johnson was adamant in telling us that managing a baseball team must differ based on the team you have. If you have homerun hitters in the lineup you focus on the long ball, if you have speed in your lineup you call for a running game, and if you have your ace pitching, well, you make sure your defense stays awake! When speaking with managers like Johnson, as well as others who have been around professional baseball for decades, the art of baseball, the art of successful leadership is apparent. As much as strategy needs to change based on the lineup card each day, the manner in which managers treat their people cannot and should not change. Players need to be given respect and given opportunities for success, for without this, their dedication will falter. We need to remember, according to Johnson, "Whatever level they're at, they earned the right to be at that level and you need to respect them and to trust them."

Pregame Prep

What motivates each of us has been studied extensively in the literature, with managers, leaders, and people at all levels trying to determine what it is that gets people to perform to their peak. According to some there are needs which people are trying to satisfy. According to others, there are inner drives which motivate actions, and others state that there are external incentives or pressures which encourage behaviors. To bring the concept of motivation to simple terms, let's relate it to something that psychologist Sigmund Freud proposed many years ago; in its simplest form, people seek to gain pleasure and avoid pain. If you do something and it feels good you will try to do it again, and if you do something and it causes pain, you will try to avoid it. It is important for us to understand here that everyone is different, and are motivated by different things; everyone looks for different things from their manager, and wants and needs something different from their leader. People derive pleasure and pain from different stimuli, and thus to be successful we need to know what makes our people *want* to work.

I think first, they get to know me, what I'm like, how I like to prepare to go into the game. Whether I like to be talked to, whether they know if they can correct me or make an adjustment while I'm warming up to go into the game. Whether they just need to be quiet and just kinda, you know, let me do my thing.

Jason Frasor, pitcher, Toronto Blue Jays

As we said, this isn't rocket science, but for many it may as well be. Sometimes managers in both the for-profit and non-profit world don't take the time or put in the necessary effort for this vital *Base of Leadership*; you need to get to know your people! Whether it is a promotion that an employee is after, a contract that a player in his last year of a contract is seeking, a good balance between work and play, or that coveted batting title which the All Star is striving for; for each player, each employee, or each volunteer, there are different drivers, and for each of these people there are also different possible de-motivators, and it's up to the manager to know what these are and to help his or her people reach their potential.

When managers outside of baseball are asked what it is that motivates them to come to work each day they often say that it is challenging work, a feeling that they are contributing to something special, or the fact that they have control over their day (albeit sometimes not as much as they would like). Many managers, when asked what drives their employees to work their hardest, respond with the simple answer, money. There's a disconnect here, in many instances managers just don't know their people. The truth is that money is important; we all know that we need to survive and would like to thrive, and money gives us a means to do that. That said, money isn't what makes us work harder, smarter, or better, it is simply the carrot that gets us to show up to work. What makes people work harder is not money, it's empowerment, it's wanting to be there and wanting to succeed (both as individuals and as a collective). Think about it, if you were offered a raise in salary would that raise cause you to work harder in six months? Are the players with the largest contracts the ones who consistently work the hardest? The simple answer is 'no'. What makes people work harder and smarter, and empowers people to push their hardest is the feeling of belonging, the feeling that they are a valued contributor, and the feeling that they are appreciated for all they do. Each player on a team will certainly find their validation in different ways; some thrive being left alone while some want a pat on the back; some want to be critiqued for their performance while others need to figure it out for themselves. It's funny to think like this, but a manager, in order to be successful, needs to have a spreadsheet (either literally or figuratively) of each player and how they each respond to different stimuli and how each react to different situations. Even though players need to be treated differently in order to be most engaged and successful, it is important once again to reiterate that each also have to be treated the same. Brad Mills, manager of the Houston Astros expressed it eloquently to us, "the way I talk to guys is different, but at the same time the theme is the same."

When guys are going through things, if they're not working, it's a different area. You gotta let them know, 'hey, you're not doing well.' I understand that you struggle, but I don't understand struggling if you don't work on it, if you don't put in time to get better. And so there's two sides to that coin: you've got to be understanding with guys and patient with guys, as long as they're giving you their best effort and they're getting ready to play. I have an understanding of all that.

Don Mattingly, manager, Los Angeles Dodgers

A Pat on the Back or a Slap in the Butt

Players and managers in all the clubhouses we visited echoed the sentiment that what they feel is a quality of a Major League (and minor league) manager is that the manager needs to take the time to get to know them. Whether it is knowing when to challenge the player with a new role, knowing when to come down hard on them for making an error, or knowing when to let them think about an error they made on their own, it is vital that the manager know the right way to react to them. Players told us that they look to their managers to help keep them focused, to keep them from "fighting against themselves" (Chris Snyder, catcher, Houston Astros), and to keep them engaged. Don Mattingly, an All Star who played in the Majors for 13 years and is now managing the Los Angeles Dodgers, is someone who sees the value in knowing his players. He explained to us that because he has been through the many stages of a baseball career as a player, he understands these stages and the priorities and issues which each stage brings with it. Mattingly and the other managers we spoke to take note of the family situations of their players, know the ups and downs that they will experience, and try to empathize with all that they are going through. It's from this understanding and empathy that a focus on being fair and equitable with players emerges.

> *You manage it one player at a time... each guy I try to connect with individually, [each guy] I try to understand individually.*
>
> **Joe Maddon, manager, Tampa Bay Rays**

Veteran infielder Omar Vizquel was adamant when talking with us that some of the players that he has played with need a manager with a laid back style whereas others respond to managers who have a 'loud and firm voice'; a notion that is not unlike management and leadership in any organization. Understanding and knowing which players respond to what style is key to the development of the relationship and in turn key to the result which will be achieved. As we've discussed at other points in this book, Tampa Bay Rays manager Joe Maddon has a unique style of leadership with a focus on fun and individuality, encouraging his players to be themselves on and off the field. MLB Network Radio host Mike Ferrin shared with us that when he enters the clubhouse of the Rays (and he spends time in lots of major league clubhouses) the clubhouse always is a fun and comfortable place to be, an observation that we too had during our time spent in their clubhouse. The lighthearted but focused clubhouse is certainly testament to Maddon's style of leadership which includes encouraging players to express themselves however they see fit. He called this "the freedom issue", and explained, "if you're a position player, I want you to run hard to first base, if you're a pitcher I want you to work on your defense more than is normal. Otherwise, you can dress how you want. If you want to wear an earring, I really don't care. If you have little quirks, all that stuff doesn't bother me." When you're on the field or preparing to get on the field you need to be serious and prepare to win; when you're not, have fun, be comfortable, and continue to think about winning!

You need to always have the players' best interests at heart because their best interest helps the ball club.
Don Mattingly, manager, Los Angeles Dodgers

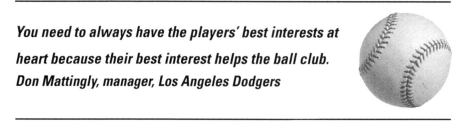

It is important for managers to always focus on not only the organization's best interest, but also that of the player as well as that, in turn will also benefit the team. The player's 'best interest', as Dodger's manager Don Mattingly pointed to during our interview with him, is going to differ from player to player. It is important for both the individual player, and the team as a whole, that the manager understands what the player's best interest is, and what the player is aiming to achieve each day, and also for each season. Relief pitcher Craig Breslow reflected about his first Spring Training with the Red Sox and how his former manager Terry Francona needed to understand the different needs and drives of his players in order to help them achieve their potential individually and collectively, "there were some veterans on the team, guys like Curt Schilling who were there to get their work in, to get ready for the season. Other guys, myself included, I was trying to make an impression. I didn't really have a chance of making the team but I signed as a minor league free agent with an invitation to spring training and that was the first time that I was going to throw in front of Terry Francona, in front of Theo Epstein, and in front of John Farrell[3], the pitching coach. So I think as a manager, if you can understand that this, spring training means something different for each player, then you probably have to treat each player differently also."

The power of knowing your players, of knowing your people, of understanding the different things that motivate them, transcends from baseball and into successful organizations and all parts of our lives. Harvard Professor Linda Hill and her co-author Kent Lineback discuss this leadership approach in their book: *Being the Boss: The 3 Imperatives for Becoming a Great Leader.* They point to the need for leaders to know their people in order to put them in the right positions, assign them the right responsibilities, and be able to delegate to them tasks which best capitalize on their strengths and interests. As we mentioned previously, Jim Collins is quoted as saying, we need to get the right people on the bus, and get the right people in the right seats. A player who doesn't fit the culture of one team might fit in very well on another. Cy Young winner David Price has said that he wouldn't pitch for the Yankees because of their facial hair rule (the Steinbrenner's don't like facial hair), whereas others like Johnny Damon and Kevin Youkilis have had no problem shaving their locks to put on pinstripes. As Collins said the right people on the right bus in the right seat!

In *knowing our people* we must not only be concerned with the motivations they hold, but also with their skills and abilities. While in

---

[3] John Farrell was interviewed for *Lead Me Out to the Ballgame* when he was manager of the Toronto Blue Jays. In 2013 Farrell became Breslow's manager when he was 'traded' to the Red Sox prior to the season for infielder Mike Aviles.

many cases the manager's job is to find ways to continue to develop their people, in some cases the skills are there, and the player just needs to be reminded of that. Consider the case of David Ortiz, All Star Designated Hitter for the Boston Red Sox, who shared with us a story about when in 2009 his season didn't start as successfully as it had in the past. Ortiz, aka Big Papi, the all-time hits leader as a designated hitter, recounted for us how when he was having difficulty and was uncomfortable with his performance that he went to his manager Terry Francona for advice. Papi told us, "I remember this one time I came to him and I said to him 'Hey Tito, what do you think I'm doing wrong?' and he said 'I don't know, I hit .125[4] when I played, so what can I tell you? Just keep on fighting big dog, just keep on doing your thing; you will come out of it.' And believe it or not, that gave me so much confidence, and next thing I knew, I was out of it."

To bring out the best in someone with experience and capabilities we sometimes just need to remind them of who they are and let them know that *we* know who they are and have confidence in their abilities. Francona's jovial response that he was not the level of player of his All Star was a way to remind David Ortiz that he is BIG PAPI and just needs to go out there and play like he always has. Has this happened to you? Have you ever been in a situation at work where you questioned your abilities in a situation? True, sometimes you need to go to the batting cage and take some extra swings, but other times you simply need to be reminded that you are capable of getting yourself out of your slump and know what you need to do to be successful. Hold up a mirror and remember you deserve to be where you are.

---

[4] Actually in his ten year major league career Terry Francona was a.274 hitter, significantly better than .125.

An All-Star at Every Position

There is a common philosophy that parents often relay to their children and managers often relay to their employees...be the best at everything you do. Well, let's think about this, can we really be the best at *everything* we do? Can we hit the most homeruns, steal the most bases, and also hit the most line drives? For most everyday players they aren't able to be the best at all of these (there are only so many Miguel Cabrera's in the world!). A more fitting philosophy is one which we believe to be more effective is to become the best at those things you are good at and get to a point where you can get by for all the other things. This philosophy works in business, where we need to know not only our strengths, but also our weaknesses, so that we can surround ourselves with people who are strong where we are not. We can't do it all ourselves and thus we need to create a team where all our 'needs' are met. The most successful managers in baseball understand this concept and work with their General Managers and owners to not only get the right people on the bus, but get them into the right seats. Veteran managers like Davey Johnson and Bobby Cox (who retired in 2010 as manager of the Atlanta Braves) are known to be masters of this, and this has certainly adding to their success. These former managers realized that to be successful with today's generation of players they needed to change with the times and become more focused on the players' situations. Former General Manager and current MLB Network Radio host Jim Duquette identified to us that Bobby Cox was one of the best at creating an environment for young players to be developed and introduced into the major leagues. The transition from the minor leagues to the major leagues is difficult, and having the support of the manager is one of the keys to the development of the rookie player. As Davey Johnson recounted for us when discussing his style of leadership, "the old dictator style of leadership has gone out with the dark ages, and I'm pretty much a dinosaur now being the oldest manager here actively. I guess leadership is, as a major league manager, being aware of the players' situation. You know where he is, what's going on with him. You know when something's distracting, and you're trying to eliminate anything that would not allow him to be as good as he can be. That awareness to me is a good leadership quality." A leader's job is to protect their people, to shield them when possible so that they can achieve success.

He [Davey Johnson] really takes the time to get to know what makes you tick ,your strengths and weaknesses on the field.

Mark DeRosa, outfielder,
Washington Nationals

The significance of 'knowing your people' can be seen in all of our lives. Consider the case of a small delivery service in Long Island, New York, where in addition to employees, there were many independent contractors delivering packages throughout the region. Each of these contractors were different, each motivated by different things, and each working for different reasons. When dealing with independent contractors who can accept or deny work at will it is important to understand those things that motivate and engage them, and it is important to understand what it is that drives them to work optimally each day. An example of the significance of knowing your people came one Friday evening when a package needed to be delivered from the suburbs of Long Island, into the hustle of New York City. Those of you who have spent time in New York on a Friday evening can understand that driving there, having to park your car (well, double or triple park it), and make a delivery, is not something that many would *want* to do. In order to assure that their packages would be delivered the owners of the company needed to use finesse in approaching their contractors; they needed to know their people. For some people an offer of extra compensation would entice them to take on the job, while for others an appeal to their commitment and their care for the organization would do the trick. If, however, the wrong technique were utilized then the packages would remain undelivered. In approaching certain drivers and offering extra compensation many drivers would respond that they were not interested, indicating that money was not their primary motivator. If these same drivers were told that the job was for an important client, and their help was needed so as to keep the customer happy, these same drivers would often complete the job. If this second approach, appealing to the loyalty the aforementioned drivers felt to the customers, was attempted with some of the other contractors the response might be quite negative, and would often include some of the language you can imagine hearing in a Major League Baseball clubhouse, with the final words including, "why don't you just go do it yourself." Alternatively, if these same drivers were told they would get paid extra for completing the job in a timely manner, they would be out the door before the sentence was finished. Our lesson here, which is reiterated throughout the chapter is that we need to know our people, we need to know what it is that makes them work, what it is that makes them perform, and know what it is that drives them to success for themselves and in turn the team they are on.

Knowing your people can be seen in contract negotiations between Fortune 100 companies as well as in our personal lives when we try to convince a friend or colleague to go to a certain restaurant for dinner; when we know what is important to them we know how to engage them and to encourage them in the direction we desire. As Dwight D. Eisenhower said, "Leadership is the art of getting someone else to do something you want done because he wants to do it."

Managing Generation Y

Walking into a Major League clubhouse in 2012 was an eye opening experience. There were a few newspapers spread around tables (although most of them remained neatly stacked and untouched), a few conversations being had about cities people visited, family, and even politics, and a consistent flow of players walking in and out of the room. What was most evident (and eye opening) as we walked around the clubhouse was that most of the players weren't interacting with each other, but rather were sitting quietly at their lockers texting, emailing, and playing *Words with Friends*. Thinking more about this, it should not come as a surprise as the majority of players in Major League Baseball today come from Generation Y (also known as Millennials), and were born between 1980 and 2000.

In the workplace there are mainly three 'generations' of people, the Baby Boomers, born between 1946 and 1964, Generation X, born between 1965 and 1979, and Generation Y (the Millennials), born between 1980 and 2000. Each of these cohorts is different as each has been reared with different historical events, different parenting styles, and different school and work experiences. The generations have been thoroughly researched and many books about how to manage and lead them written. Some of the work on these generations comes from author Bruce Tulgan[13] who posits that more so than previous generations, the millennials are a group that wants to be given an abundance of training, wants to feel a part of a team, wants to receive ongoing feedback, and wants to know today what tomorrow will bring. Past generations tended to be more focused on the day to day and working towards their goals step by step whereas the millennials want to be given a roadmap for the future. Is this group, whether on a baseball field or in a traditional workplace harder to manage and lead? No. Absolutely not. They are simply different and the difficulty arises when managers don't realize that. What the millennials need most is support, as Ned Yost, Kansas City Royals manager told us, managers need to pay attention to all the expectations that are being put on the younger players from the coaching staff, their teammates, and even the fans, and help them to learn ways to deal with these expectations and use them to develop.

> *There's times where we try to set the expectations*
> *up higher. You gotta be able to look at them and know*
> *when to ramp them up and know when to back them*
> *down because you put too much on them.*
> **Ned Yost, manager, Kansas City Royals**

Players, like employees of the millennial generation seek feedback and desire to have the actions of their managers explained to them. This, in the business world as well as in baseball, is not always possible, and not always acted upon. Pitcher, Brad Lidge, not a member of the millennial generation, explained how younger players can be insecure about moves that managers make in the game, and appreciate when they receive reinforcement and positive feedback from them. Younger players can be nervous about making mistakes and thinking that if they make one they may not be on the field for the next game. As Lidge told us, "you don't want that kind of unsettled feeling. Of course, the more you get in the game you realize that's not necessarily true, but as a younger player you don't really know that. So if you have a manager that's reinforcing things, it goes a long way." In the workplace, as well as on the diamond, it is useful for managers to understand the dynamics of the different generations, to understand the extra support that the younger generation seeks. In some places there is resentment for this, but an important point is that if we want our people to succeed we need to not fight against them, but use their differences to become strengths. Managers need to understand that support and validation need to be coupled with challenge and encouragement. Players, as most from the millennial generation, want the message reinforced that if they work hard they will succeed. Matt Sinatro, a long time coach for many major league teams, shared with us a bit about the relationship he had with some young players who have since become stars. As Sinatro told us when talking about players who he worked with as youngsters like David Wright, Craig Biggio, Ken Caminiti, and others, "we always knew that we were there for one reason, for them to get better." When the focus is on the goal and everyone understands that they are working towards the same objective, success will come.

Leaders on the Field

One of the things a successful leader in all walks of life will do is know how to best utilize his or her players. They will know that someone like Ricky Romero of the Toronto Blue Jays is not a "big vocal guy" as he told us, but he does "work hard in the weight room and on the mound, and all that stuff speaks for itself to a manager." Romero's work ethic and focus are his way of leading by example, and he is someone who was recognized by his former manager, John Farrell, as one of the leaders on the team. Another leader identified by Farrell on the 2012 Toronto Blue Jays was veteran Jose Bautista, who, because of his experience and intelligence, could serve as a sounding board for his managers, help them to understand the pulse of the clubhouse, and identify any issues which need addressing. It is vital in today's organizations for leaders to understand that leadership and organizational or team success is not about one person, it is about everyone taking ownership of their actions.

In order for optimal levels of success to be achieved leaders must be found in all the ranks and throughout every part of the organization. In the case of the Toronto Blue Jays it was expressed to us by Farrell that it was fortunate for them to have two of their best players as leaders, and fortunate that these two players were on 'both sides of the game', a pitcher and an everyday player. This was an interesting and meaningful point in that people tend to look to others who do the 'same job' as they do; it is good to make sure that there is a champion for your cause and a model of appropriate and successful behavior in all areas of the organization so as to set the right tone throughout. To be most successful an organization must have its messages and goals vocalized not just by the formal leaders, but by the informal leaders throughout as well.

> ***There's some of the veterans in here that's taught me, whether it's toning it out, or just by exuding confidence.***
>
> **Logan Schafer, outfielder, Milwaukee Brewers**

We've spoken quite a bit about the motivational aspects of knowing your people, but in baseball, as well as in other industries and parts of our life, we also need to know our people so as to get the *hot bat*[5] in the game. We see this as managers will play their backup players for a stretch when they are hot, often serving a dual purpose of giving some much needed rest to an everyday player as well as empowering our backups. We see this in other industries, such as sales, that when an agent closes numerous deals and are 'on a streak', they will be given lead after lead. Former General Manager and current MLB radio and TV personality Jim Duquette shared with us a bit about a manager, San Francisco Giants manager Bruce Bochy, who he felt did a great job of "playing the hot hand" when he managed (and won) the World Series in 2010. Duquette explained that Bochy wouldn't be married to certain roles, he would go with a player who was hot, give them a short leash, and put his faith in them to deliver.

To be successful a manager must understand not just the temperament and needs of his or her people, but also the ways that those characteristics work with the skills the person has and the situation that the team or organization is in. This leads us to a more in depth discussion of *Knowing the Game* which will be explored in Chapter 8.

---

[5] In baseball, a player with a hot bat is someone who has been getting more hits than usual over an extended period of time.

A trip to the mound...

- Do I know why the members of my team come to work each day?

- How can I better capitalize on the individual strengths of my team?

- Am I spending enough time learning about my team members and how to keep them focused and performing to their potential?

- Have I done enough research on managing different generations and different types of personalities so as to be the best leader I can be?

- Is the feedback I provide to my team members developmental?

Chapter 5
Cultivate Relationships

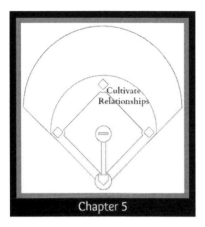

It seems like good managers have good relationships with their players.

Mike McCoy, infielder, Toronto Blue Jays

A popular TV show, based on our primal need for relationships, started in 1982 and ran successfully for eleven years, Cheers. The premise of the sitcom was that a former Boston Red Sox pitcher, Sam Malone (played by Ted Danson) opens a bar in Boston and its popularity can be summed up by a line from the show's theme, "You wanna go where everybody knows your name." In the most basic terms, relationships (love and belonging) are the level three needs on Maslow's hierarchy of needs. The most fundamental needs that Maslow identified as motivational drivers of people are physiological (food, water, air), followed by safety (job, family, health), and then relationships...once people have food, water, and safety, they are motivated by forming relationships. With the need for relationships so primal, it is not surprising that to be an effective leader requires the ability to build meaningful relationships with those around us.

Ned Yost, manager of the Kansas City Royals and Brad Mills, manager of the Houston Astros each take time every day to talk with their players. Whether that is a full conversation, a simple hello, or an encouraging talk for those who may have had a rough day, making the time is important. Mills shared with us that he really wants to "know more about them and their family, and talk about if they're playing golf or if they hunt." He wants "to be able to form some type of relationship with them." The efforts by managers in spending time speaking with their players does not go unnoticed, as Bud Norris of the Astros told us, "when he takes the time to go out there and really get to know [us] on that personal level and talk to [us], it's pretty important."

Building relationships is an important skill for effective leadership. People typically leave an organization because of an issue with people (usually the manager) more often than with the company itself or because of monetary issues. A common reason that leaders fail is because they are either unwilling or unable to build meaningful relationships or create a thriving team environment. Like any skill worth acquiring it takes dedication, discipline, and a focused effort to develop. However, once you have developed this skill, you will reap the rewards of relationship-based leadership as you will find increased engagement with your team, higher levels of trust and communication, and an openness that fosters progress and development.

In this chapter, we will focus on four areas or practices that help to build meaningful relationships in the workplace. First, you must invest the time with people. It is through the time that you invest with others that the relationships begin to develop. Second, it is important that we get to know our people. Taking a personal interest in people will assist with creating sustainable relationships. Third, becoming an empathetic leader enables us to understand the needs of others and gain appreciation for them. Finally, by becoming someone who is relatable, we communicate our human side and can show others how to balance strength and vulnerability.

Time is an Investment

Most leaders start their day with a rather large to do list that is likely filled with meetings, projects, and other appointments that are necessary but perhaps not mission centric. We often end the day wondering why we were not able to spend time on what truly matters, on the things that will make a long-term difference to our organization. When you get right down to it, you aren't a leader without people around you, and people require time. It is through the time that you spend with others that understanding grows and relationships begin to form.

Pitcher Craig Breslow discussed with us the difficulty and struggles that he faced during the 2011 season. Even though 2011 wasn't a bad season for him statistically, Breslow knew it wasn't on par with his previous work and wasn't the caliber of work he felt he should have accomplished. Breslow's performance in 2011 coincided with a managerial change on his team, the Oakland A's, which had an impact on his playing time and the situations he was used in as a relief pitcher. Breslow's situation is not unique in baseball and not unique in the world in general. When managerial changes occur there is often an impact on players or employees as new relationships must be established and new expectations and philosophies understood. Breslow noted that his new manager, Bob Melvin, helped ease the leadership transition tremendously, noting , "I felt like when Bob Melvin took over, he did his best and made an effort to meet every player, to talk to them, to tell them what he expected of them and where he saw them fitting in." This is a terrific example for others to follow when coming into a new role, forming relationships early has a lasting and profound impact on your team and its success.

Breslow's example above points to the need for new managers to take the time to get to know their players and the value they bring to the table. Doing this at the onset of the relationship, however, is certainly not enough. Spending time with people is an investment that every leader needs to make as it helps to create a greater understanding and appreciation for both parties, and with that understanding and appreciation comes an attitude of increased engagement and in turn performance. Zach Duke, of the Houston Astros, appreciated how his previous manager on the Arizona Diamondbacks, Kirk Gibson, always made an effort to understand his people. He accurately noted that so much of leadership is managing personalities and that this ability comes from spending time with your people. Brad Mills expressed to us that spending time with his players was a key leadership behavior. He said, "I try to spend a little time with each guy each day, and that's hard, and sometimes you don't make it...the majority of guys at least, I was able to at least say hi to today, pat them on the back, or let them know at least I'm thinking about them." Travis Schlichting of the Oakland A's noted how important it is to feel comfortable with your manager, and that "just being able to hold a normal conversation with your manager and not feel intimidated," also helps to create an atmosphere of mutual respect.

There's always time during the day, usually it's during batting practice. We see the manager walking around the outfield and maybe talk to the players. We're not saying 15 minute conversations, like 5 minutes, not every day, but just every now and then. Just let them know 'hey, I'm still thinking about you.'
Darren Oliver, pitcher, Toronto Blue Jays

A common concern of managers in industry is that they should not develop friendships with their employees as a separation is, in their minds needed. The fact is, however, that we spend more time with our coworkers than we do with our family, and this is especially true in the world of Major League Baseball. Becoming friends with coworkers can make work a more pleasant environment and can even increase performance through a heightened sense of satisfaction and the desire to never let your teammates or your manager down. The important thing to remember as the leader of a team is that the focus of the professional side of the relationship needs to be goal-oriented, and team members must be held accountable. Having direct and honest conversations regarding the accountability of our people will go more smoothly when there is a collegial relationship based on mutual respect and understanding, as well as a greater commitment to one another.

Many of the players we spoke with talked to us about how much they enjoy spending time in the off-season with other players and managers; they talked about the family that is Major League Baseball. There were many tales about hunting and fishing trips, who caught the biggest fish, or who was the best shot when deer hunting. Sometimes a round of golf was enjoyed or a day of surfing the waves. Washington Nationals pitcher, Tyler Clippard, discussed how important such activities are to building a personal relationship and to having a sense of comfort on a team, "we went and played golf on an off day," Clippard told us, "and he [Davey Johnson] was there, and our pitching coach was there and there were maybe six of us players and we all played golf together. I think being able to do that was pretty cool." Pretty cool and also quite useful in developing bonds between players as well as coaches and managers.

It is important to recognize that the personal lives of your team members are important. You can build your relationship by taking the time to celebrate birthdays, weddings, and the birth of their children. As you lead in this area, you will find that your team members will start doing the same with their teammates, and the bond will help increase the effectiveness of the entire team. During the off-season, prior to the 2011 season, Brad Mills, determined it would be beneficial to spend time bonding with the Astros veteran outfielder, Carlos Lee.

He shared this story, "Last year, I took a trip down to Panama to visit Carlos [Lee], and spent about three or four days down there with him. I just felt that it was important. Calling and talking to guys in the off season is important. Not to check up on them and ask them if they're working out, and not acting like a policeman, but just saying, 'hey, just kind of wondering where your mind is. Are you thinking about the team? Are you thinking about getting in shape? What's going through your mind? What's the process, where are you at in getting ready for spring training or whatever.' And then take it from there." Spending time with Lee was not only about preparing for the season physically, it was about helping him prepare for the season mentally, helping him to know he is valued and needed as a veteran to be a leader on his team.

It's important to remember that the time you spend with your people is truly an investment. People need to know that you are human and that you also face challenges. They need to believe that you understand them and appreciate the work that they do. As we've said, without people around you, you cannot lead.

Get to Know Them

Back in the 80's there was a hot topic in management – management by walking around (MBWA), a term that was popularized in 1982 by Tom Peters and Robert Waterman in their book, *In Search of Excellence*[14]. The basic premise was that leaders need to get off the phone and out of their offices, and walk around the workplace so they can get a true feel for what is really happening. Instead of reading a report or sending an email leaders who practice MBWA are able to speak to employees first hand and observe challenges that they may be facing as well as identify innovative ideas. Steve Jobs was a huge proponent of MBWA and he was able to effectively use this approach not only with employees but also with customers at Apple.

The concept of managing by walking around was mentioned during our interviews with Major League Baseball managers and players. Bud Norris, pitcher for the Houston Astros, commented on this specifically, "He [the manager] takes time to come out during batting practice and really walk out and around the outfield and talk to all the guys, just kind of check in. If somebody's got something they bring up they need to talk to him about, he'll give you the opportunity to really talk about it. But he's out there; really giving himself the opportunity during batting practice to come meet all the guys, talk to the guys at the back end, the bullpen. When he takes the time to go out there and really get to know [his pitchers] on that personal level and talk to them, it's pretty important."

Padres manager, Bud Black, identified Dusty Baker as someone he learned managerial skills from, and often seeks to emulate. Black stated that he appreciated Baker's energy, "his enthusiasm, his being able to connect with players on a personal level." Interestingly, the Astros Scott Moore also used Dusty Baker as an example, "He's really good at knowing a lot about his players. He knows family things, he knows background of players, and for me, I think that makes you feel good when you come into a place and your manager's taking the time to know things about you other than just what you do on the baseball field. I think that makes you show up to the field every day excited and wanting to perform. I think that's an important thing for sure."

As you see, developing relationships was a popular area of discussion in the interviews we conducted. Sportswriter Tom Boswell mentioned that the manager of the Washington Nationals, Davey Johnson, always takes the time to get to know his players personally. Brad Mills felt that it is important as a manager to be able to form some type of relationship with his players. Similarly, Neil Wagner of the A's felt that taking a personal interest makes a huge difference in how he relates to his manager. Ryan Kalish of the Boston Red Sox discussed this attribute regarding his former manager Terry Francona, and current manager, Bobby Valentine, "you just talk and people are nice and they want to know about your family, they want to understand who you are so that they can help you be a better baseball player, and even help you off the field. As far as big league managers go, I've played for Terry Francona, he's very good about that, Bobby's already been really good about that, and I look down to the minor leagues, Marty Baylor, all those guys; you just sit in their office and just talk life. That for me is something. If I were to manage, that's what I would do. I'd make sure I get to know my players for more than what they are on the field."

Mike Scioscia, manager of the Los Angeles Angels, mentioned that one of the most important things for a leader to do is to connect with players, and to connect to their passion. He told us, "Sometimes I break down the barriers talking to them here [in the clubhouse], and that translates on the field where the trust is developed. When you get to know them as a person you connect with their passion. There's not a player in that room that doesn't love the game, if they didn't, they wouldn't be at this level. They love it, and they live it. And once you connect with that, it's a great bond. It helps you to steer them in the right direction."

Whether you are a little league coach, a major league manager, a line supervisor, a non-profit director, a teacher, or a CEO, management by walking around will enable you to become closer to your team, form more meaningful relationships, and gain a clearer understanding of what is happening with your team, thus, reducing surprises. It's important not to allow technology to limit your use of MBWA and getting to know your people. Yes, it is pretty simple to send an email or distribute a memo but actual face time with people is where the relationships are built. To be most effective at getting to know people and achieving positive results with MBWA, there are several things to keep in mind. First, you need to do it regularly so it becomes a natural process; it needs to become part of your routine and thus part of the organizational culture. When talking with people, be sure to keep an open mind, be an active listener, and ask for suggestions to engage them in the conversation. If the other party has suggestions or concerns it is important to follow up in a reasonable amount of time, if you open the door by asking for opinions or issues, it's important to acknowledge them. Remember, when 'walking around' in your role as a leader, this is not the time for criticism or performance management, meetings can be set up to wear your managerial hat, 'walking around' is a time for leadership, not management. Finally, allow yourself to be known as much as you want to know your team because relationships are mutual and if you are not open with your people you cannot expect your people to be open with you.

Be Empathetic

As we continue our discussion regarding relationship-driven leadership, it is important to note that such leaders are patient and tolerant; they are more empathetic than others. As we discussed in Chapter 2, the importance of values and leading by example cannot be understated as empathetic leaders use values to guide them in a more subjective approach to decision-making. Additional hallmarks of this type of leader are that they typically build consensus and seek to achieve harmony within their teams. It is not unusual for empathetic leaders to ask for constructive feedback or to admit when they are wrong. It takes a big person and an exemplary leader to be able to admit his or her mistakes and realize that things that were done could have been done differently. This is exactly what A's manager Bob Melvin did when he realized that he didn't utilize relief pitcher Craig Breslow to his potential at the end of the 2011 season. Breslow recounted for us a bit about this situation, it is evident that it had a profound impact on his view of his then manager, Bob Melvin. Breslow told us, "as the season played out, I wasn't really being used kind of in the situations we had talked about and he made it a point to come up to me late in the season and say that he felt like I was the one guy that maybe he had kind of let down. And that it was his job to empower me and to instill confidence in me based on what I meant to the team and what I had done for the team in the past. And he felt like he had kind of let me down and that he hadn't done that. He was going to make an effort for the last couple weeks of the season to try and use me in higher leverage situations and kind of get me back to where I was. And as a credit to him, he did. And it ended up working out pretty well. I had a better September than August, July or June."

It is no wonder that many of us gravitate toward leaders who are empathetic. Such leaders have meaningful relationships with their teams, are typically more satisfying to work with, and they are able to enhance performance as well.[15] This is at the heart of the concept introduced in 1995 by Daniel Goleman when he expressed that we needed more than a high IQ to be successful; we need to be emotionally intelligent as well.[15] Emotional intelligence involves four attributes, two of which were touched upon in Chapter 2, self-awareness and self-management. The other attributes are social awareness and relationship management. A quote from John Doone comes to mind, "No man is an island."[16] This still remains true today; in baseball, in business, and in life.

> *He [the manager] has to care about his players; that way they will follow.*
>
> **Bruce Chen, pitcher, Kansas City Royals**

Through empathy, we are better able to understand the needs of other people and appreciate what they may be going through. The insights that leaders gain through this trait can help us understand how others may react, or perhaps what they are feeling about a particular situation. High performing employees, volunteers, and players are often very competitive, have extremely high standards for their performance, and will push to the limit of their performance capabilities. Andrew Bailey, pitcher for the Boston Red Sox, discussed this with us and how important it is for managers to ask people how they are feeling, and if they might benefit from a day off. He noted that highly competitive people want to be in the game every day and might need someone to empathize and make a rest decision for them. Bailey shared, "I think for a reliever, we always want the ball, always want to be out in the field, but I think it's imperative that a manager sometimes override that and do what's healthy, what's right for the player. If you've gone three days in a row and you've thrown a lot of pitches, you may need a day off and I think instead of asking a player they kind of just tell them, 'Hey look, you're off today.' That's how relationships work." The ability to know when to make that decision and tell the player (or other direct report) to take some time off comes through understanding them, recognizing the work that they do, and being able to empathize enough to take the pressure off of them for the good of the individual as well as the good of the team.

By developing empathy, leaders gain many advantages. Innovation is more likely because there is a safer environment and thus taking risks feels safe because there is little fear of blame or reprisal for taking a chance with something new. Having empathy helps us to understand our team members; helping us to identify causes of poor performance as well as helping our people improve and even exceed expectations. Helping others work through the difficult times and work through their struggles was a sentiment echoed in our clubhouse interviews by current players, managers, and retired players. Michael Taylor, outfielder for the Oakland A's, shared with us, "the best managers I've ever had are the ones that remember. 'You know what, I remember back when I played what it was like to go through a slump. I remember what it was like to doubt myself. I remember what it's like when I was riding high.'"

Similarly, Ron Gardenhire, manager of the Minnesota Twins, stated that, "I think the one thing that has helped me probably the most is to remember what it was like to be a player. That's very important. You remember what they're going through. You think back when you played and how hard it was and the things you struggled with and, you know what, when you see something happen on the field, you can always say, 'I've been there,' or 'I know what he feels like right now.' And you try to look at it from the player's side and work your way from there. When you forget that, it gets a little tough, you forget how hard the game is."

Corporate America is embracing empathetic leaders more readily because of seeing the success that such leaders have on their organizations. Bill Hewlett (co-founder of Hewlett-Packard) was known to walk the floors and truly listen to employee concerns. Southwest Airlines founder, Herb Kelleher, and CEO Gary Kelly thrive on creating a culture that is built on heart and being empathetic to employees and customers. Continued bottom line performance of such organizations is causing others to take note and realize that being empathetic is no longer a nice-to-have "soft" skill for successful organizations.

When considering your propensity for empathy or even thinking about ways you can focus to improve this skill, contemplate this: First, before we can empathize we must first listen and listen attentively to what people are saying and what might be behind what they are saying. While listening, we can also take note of body language because it will often communicate thoughts and feelings more than the words being used. Smile. This seems simple but we can probably all do more of this every day because it helps others to feel comfortable with us and makes us feel great at the same time.

Relatability is Important

The final area for building relationships is being relatable or having relatability. We've talked quite a bit about how important it is for a manager to get to know his or her people; in addition, your direct reports want to know you too – they want to be able to relate to you. As noted in Chapter 3, respect is something that every leader strives to attain and being relatable makes it much easier for people to respect you and it also inspires people to be extremely loyal. Being relatable also attracts people who desire to be a part of your journey to achieve your vision because they can visualize being at that destination with you.

Ron Gardenhire stated that being able to relate to players is one of the most important aspects of being a manager. Likewise, Manny Acta, manager of the Cleveland Indians, noted that he makes an effort to know each player because he wants them to know he is like them. He said, "I'm just like you, I'm your boss, but I'm just like you. I eat and shop at the same places; I listen to the same music and wear the same clothes you do. I think that makes them feel good when they see that you're just like them." There is a fine line here between friend and boss and several of the Major League Baseball players noted that fact in their interviews. As Darin Mastroianni, Outfielder for Minnesota Twins told us, "I think a manager who gets his players, someone who can relate with us, but at the same point, be our head honcho. He's got to run the show, he is the manager. Who can relate with us and understand what we go through on a day to day basis and understand the ins and outs not only on the field but things that happen to us off the field too."

If they [managers] can relate to the players and they are in their environment, find out what makes them tick, hat is something I think the manager can do that would help.
Sean Burnett, pitcher, Washington Nationals

Leaders who are relatable tend to embrace mistakes. They use mistakes as a learning experience and often tell stories that demonstrate their own vulnerability. Retired player, Eddie Taubensee, discussed the importance of managers communicating that they understand – that they struggled when they were in the player's position too. He noted that many players have trouble thinking of their manager in a position where perhaps they really messed up or had ups and down. But when the manager is honest about his struggles, players really appreciate that because they can truly relate to their manager. Ron Gardenhire, believes in this managerial philosophy, and talked about this during our interview, "I was an infielder, so if you see a guy trying to do something a little too quick and, I'm not picking out specific players, but you see a guy really trying so stinking hard that it's actually working against him, or you see a guy miss a ball, it takes a little bit of a bad hop and maybe if his hands, you know maybe if he'd slowed down a little bit, he might of caught the ball. And you think back, you know, I've done that, I did that before, I know what you went through. So for me, to be able to relate to him, it's a lot easier if I remember those things when I'm talking to him. It's actually having been there and done it. You know what, I've been there, I've swung at the slider in the dirt, I've made an error."

As we work on our ability to be more relatable, we should consider balancing strength with vulnerability. Again, demonstrating that you are human, have struggled, made mistakes but also bring in stories to show how you overcame that difficulty or how you bounced back from a poor decision or less than stellar performance. Determine what you are comfortable with and then share some of those aspects with your team. You don't need to share everything about your personal life but it is important to share enough to create that sense of partnership and relatability. Finally, it is always a best practice to be available to your team. Leaders lead people and the only way to do that is to truly spend time together. We will dive into the communication aspects of being a leader in Chapter 7 but for now simply focusing on being available with your time and even your emotion is important to develop relatability.

Start Building Relationships Today

We have discussed that to build meaningful relationships in the workplace we must first invest the time with people and get to know them. We also need to become an empathetic leader and be someone who is relatable. But let's consider some ways that we can start building relationships today. First, it is important that you know yourself, your values, and your goals. Once you are clear with this foundation, you need to determine how to best articulate this information with clarity and enthusiasm. Next, seek to understand others – what are their skills – what are their goals – how might they align and relate to yours? Great leaders continually seek to develop their skills and that often starts with acquiring meaningful feedback. Ask others to help you identify your strengths and opportunities in the area of relationship building. Also, take time to truly analyze the relationships you have now. Determine the strengths or where you might want to build some more. Where are the gaps? Are there people with whom you currently do not have a strong relationship but perhaps you should? Make an action plan to start closing such gaps.

Sometimes the biggest changes will need to come from within – a mindset shift. For example, examine how well you open yourself to differing viewpoints or how often you seek feedback or ideas from others. How will you increase your ability to be empathic and vulnerable while still maintaining appropriate strength and decisiveness? Seek opportunities to collaborate with others, especially with people or departments where you currently may not have strong or developed relationships. Determine the best way to truly champion the development of your team. Helping others to achieve their goals is a great way to build relationships, enhance your own skills, and find your work to be much more satisfying. In all you do, take time to show appreciation for others and thank them for their feedback, time, and contributions. The important thing is that you determine that building relationships is important for your success and something that you truly desire to do. If that is your decision, then there is no time like the present to make it happen!

A trip to the mound...

- What are the goals of each of my team members?

- How much one-on-one time to I spend with each member of my team?

- Am I able to easily engage in a personal conversation with each team member?

- When was the last time I sought feedback or admitted to a mistake with my team?

- How can I more effectively use my strength and vulnerability to become more relatable?

Chapter 6
Support Your People

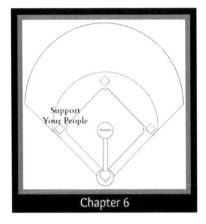

When you know that a manager has your back, you'll have his. You want to play for him, you want to show up every day and give it your best, you want to play hurt, and you want to do all that for your manager.

Ryan Doumit, catcher, Minnesota Twins

"I've got your back" or "He has my back" – how many times do we hear that? It is certainly not a new sentiment. During the Revolutionary War, Benjamin Franklin observed that "we can hang together, or hang separately." In group combat situations it is not uncommon to use a back to back stance to quickly react to attacks from different directions. Even in the movie "Gladiator" three of the gladiators form a team because Maximus (played by Russell Crowe) rallies them with, "We can fight together or die separately." Today it has become a battle cry, so to speak, in the workplace and certainly in team sports. People want to feel that someone is there for them, supporting them, through thick and thin.

Major League Baseball players are no different. Time and time again we were told that "having our back" was one of the most important characteristics for a Major League Baseball manager to have. In a sport where trades to other teams and being sent down to the minor leagues are an ongoing occurrence throughout the long season, players felt very strongly that support and feeling that their managers had their back was critical. Adam LaRoche, infielder on the Washington Nationals, talked about how this is especially important externally, "right or wrong, if the player's right or wrong, to the media, to the public, you take their side. Obviously there are some exceptions, something blatant or whatever, but for the most part really good managers that get respected by the entire clubhouse are ones that don't mind jumping on a grenade for a player once in a while." Joe Mauer, All-Star catcher for the Minnesota Twins, agreed that it is important that managers demonstrate to their players that "you have their back, really in any situation." Having support from a manager builds confidence in players as well as in people outside of the Game. As Clint Robinson, an infielder on the Kansas City Royals, told us, "you want to know he's going to stick up for you when the game's on the line and always be on your side. That gives you confidence as a player."

In this chapter we look at what it means to be a supportive leader and how to cultivate this important *Base of Leadership*. First, we will explore the outward signs of providing support. By demonstrating support, we communicate to others that we believe in them; building commitment, loyalty, and respect in the process. Second, it is important that we understand what it means to "have their back" and the best ways to accomplish this while continuing to maintain our values and lead by example. Third, how can we, no matter what our industry, become a players' manager? By becoming a supportive leader we instill confidence in our team, an act which can have a positive impact on performance results. Providing support has many advantages, and brings together many of the leadership dimensions that are explored throughout this book.

Signs of Support

When thinking about showing support, we should consider why we should support people as well as how to accomplish it successfully. Many of the reasons why have been discussed in earlier chapters. Demonstrating support tells people that you believe in them and this contributes to loyalty, commitment, and even respect. Actions of support also communicate that you are focused on your team more than yourself and this builds meaningful relationships. Support also comes in the form of ensuring that all team members have the tools, access, even authority necessary to execute their jobs effectively. Other times, things may not be going as planned or even poorly and it is important that – as the leader – some of the heat can be taken off of the employee and absorbed by you.

There are some games that are not going to be as hot as others and hopefully he can ride the boat with you.

Jonathan Broxton, pitcher, Kansas City Royals

As the leader, your team's success or failure will be attributed to you. Leaders are accountable when things go wrong and are praised when things go well. In fact, outcomes are the responsibility of the leader, but great leaders understand that their success or failure hinges on their ability to get things accomplished through others, not by their efforts individually. A supportive leader is satisfied to find the joy in their team's success, remain humble, and shift the praise to the team. Conversely, when the team suffers a loss, the supportive leader absorbs the heat, takes the responsibility, and avoids playing the blame game. Leading in this manner will build credibility, not only with direct reports but also with superiors.

It is not surprising that having the support of a manager was a popular topic in our interviews with Major League Baseball players. Those in the game clearly understand that their actions at the plate, on the mound, or on the field affect the outcome of a game. They also noted the impact that it has on their attitude as well as their play when they know that their manager is ready and willing to take some of that heat off of them both on the field with the umpires or opposing players, with the 'front office' (ie, the executives), and even with the media. The most respected managers are known for putting things into perspective, understanding that there are many moving parts, and recognizing that no one action truly causes the ultimate outcome of a game. Adam LaRoche, infielder with the Washington Nationals summed it up this way, "A good manager will say, 'Naw, that one's on me, I screwed that up.' Even though he knows avoiding that error would have helped, he wants to take the focus off of those guys, except to praise them. So when good things happen, a lot of times the manager won't take the credit. He'll say – 'Oh that was the guys, I was just out there watching, having fun.' When bad things happen, the manager's like – 'Oh man, I screwed that up.'"

Directing the attention and blame off of the team and focusing it on ourselves doesn't mean that we should make excuses for the players or defend them regardless of the situation, but sometimes, as Josh Willingham of the Twins told us, it's appreciated, " I think a manager gets his players trust by letting them know that they're backing you 100% whether you're right or wrong in a situation. A lot of times you do something in a baseball game where you're probably not going to be right, but your manager backs you up. Just has your back." Now, Willingham is referring to situations on the field, a blown call, a heated argument, etc. If someone does something unethical, violated company policy, or committed an act that was incongruent with the organization's values, that is another story, and not the time to go to the mat and defend them unconditionally. However, even in cases like this, it is always wise to praise in public and coach on such violations in private. Publically, as long as our player or employee is a part of our team, if we want to have their support we need to have their back.

Former manager of the Chicago White Sox and Miami Marlins, Ozzie Guillen, is often thought of as a hot-head or someone that easily blows up, especially with the media. Mike Ferrin, of Sirius XM, talked with us a bit about Guillen and had some pretty supportive things to say. He noted that Guillen was the kind of manager who would take the pressure off of his guys, particularly in front of the media. He said, "When his team would win, he'd give all the credit to players. When they'd lose, he'd take all the time to kind of shelter them." This worked well for Ozzie and he built loyalty with his players and even won a World Series for the Chicago White Sox.

I want this guy. This is my guy. I'm going to take him with me.
Craig Breslow, pitcher, Arizona Diamondbacks

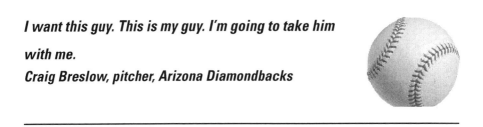

In business and in baseball, there are times when upper management wants to make personnel changes. Perhaps they see this as an opportunity to shake things up, stir the pot, or go in a new direction, especially if the organization or team has been unsuccessful or simply stagnant. This is where it is important that the manager truly understands their people and their individual and collective talents. There may be a situation that is preventing someone from performing to the best of their ability – maybe it is the external environment or it could be that all the team components needed are not yet acquired. In Major League Baseball, the General Manager may want to trade a player, send them to the minors, or simply switch up the lineup when the team needs a bit of a boost, but sometimes the manager has something else in mind. Pitcher Brad Lidge of the Washington Nationals gave an example of this when his manager said, "'I really don't care at all what anybody thinks. Period.' And simple as that he said 'I'm sticking with my guys because I know what they can do, and if everybody in the world thinks differently, I couldn't care less because I know what I think.': Similarly, Jared Saltalamacchia, Boston Red Sox catcher, discussed how he truly appreciates it when his manager sticks up for the team, "When a manager sticks up for his team, when a manager shows us he's a part of the team and not part of the front office or something like that, I think that's a big thing. We're all here together, front office included. But there's a lot of stuff the players go through as a team that the manager sees, so it's nice to have him on board." When used appropriately, showing signs of support to your team can develop relationships, and as we've pointed to, increase loyalty and respect.

Do You Have Their Backs?

We hear the phrase a lot; whether with family, friends, co-workers, or teammates, "I have your back." We like hearing it because it brings us a sense of security and we believe someone will be there for us, we are not alone, or maybe someone will catch us if we fall. In leadership, many want to be "that" leader who can say "I have your back" and truly mean it. Sometimes we worry that the situation may make it difficult to live up to the statement. But as we discussed earlier regarding leading by example, to be a truly credible leader, we must walk the talk and if we use phrases like this, we need to be able to stand behind our words as well.

Have your back out on the field. If any obvious controversy comes up, stick up for your players

Ryan Sweeney, outfielder, Boston Red Sox

The concept of fairness and due process comes to mind when thinking about having someone's back. There will always be conflict and controversy where people are concerned; however, regardless of the outcome, we desire to be treated fairly and to believe that our voice was heard and point of view registered. That is not to say that things will always go our way but it is certainly easier to accept an outcome when the process was fair and just. If you have watched a few baseball games, you have likely seen a disagreement with an umpire over a questionable call. Although this situation is much more public than what typically occurs in the business world, it is a great example that resonates with all of us. Chad Tracy, infielder with the Washington Nationals, described it this way, "You've got to feel like your manager's always got your back. You know, it's one of those things where, it doesn't matter who the player is on the team, the superstar, the 25th man on the roster, if you feel like the manager's got your back, if you're arguing with an umpire, you don't feel like you're getting fair treatment, or whatever it might be. It means a lot sometimes to just have your manager run out there, and have your back with an umpire or whatever situation it might be."

Willie Bloomquist, of the Arizona Diamondbacks, recalled an experience that he had early in his career that exemplifies the impact that supporting your people has on a player. In a game early in his career, while playing for the Kansas City Royals under manager Trey Hillman, Bloomquist felt that he was being unfairly targeted by an umpire for questioning a call he made early in the game. When he was called out on strikes for the second time he had some choice words for the umpire, here's Bloomquist's account of what happened and how Hillman had his back. "I said a few things to him [the umpire] and he told me "not another word or I'm gonna toss you." Just as I was getting ready to turn around and say [something] to him my manager was already out of the dugout, it was Trey Hillman, he was in his grill and he ended up getting tossed for me. It was pretty cool just in the fact that, I'm not superstar, wouldn't matter if it was Barry Bonds up there, he would have done the same thing.... That's pretty cool when your manager's got your back and he's ready to go to bat for you, ready to fight for you."

Bryce Harper, outfielder with the Washington Nationals, said something similar, "Just backing us up. I think that's the biggest thing about all the guys. If you're getting thrown out or you have a bad call and you argue and he's [the manager] right there doing that for you. I think that's the biggest thing about all the guys, all the players, they want that, to have their coach be there for them and let them know, 'Hey, we got your back.'"

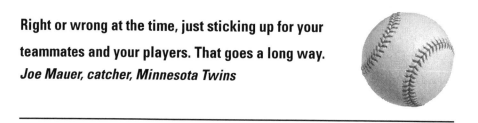

Right or wrong at the time, just sticking up for your teammates and your players. That goes a long way.
Joe Mauer, catcher, Minnesota Twins

Sometimes it can be more challenging because there is a legitimate mistake made. We all make mistakes, including our best employees. The best leaders actually embrace mistakes because it indicates that people are taking risks, trying new things, and pushing the envelope on performance. If we don't embrace and encourage this type of behavior, development will stagnate and our team's performance will level off. We must take the attitude that mistakes are part of a process and not a failure. Great leaders encourage this and create an environment that is safe to make mistakes but they also want to ensure that people learn from their mistakes, learn how to correct the problem, and take steps to avoid repeating prior mistakes. Jose Bautista, outfielder with the Toronto Blue Jays, said this in our interview, "I think the biggest thing is making sure that your guys are just trying to do their best, hoping for good results. And when those results are not there, just sticking behind your players and realizing that in baseball you can't do everything perfect and sometimes stuff just doesn't go your way."

Scott Atchison, pitcher with the Boston Red Sox, noted how this plays into really knowing your players and that other players truly take note of how a manager might stand up for a player – even if they are on another team. Here is what he shared, "I think as a manager, if you know your players, I think that's the biggest thing. And I know from a player's standpoint, the one thing most players want is their manager to back them up at all times, you know, whether they're right or wrong, it gives you a sense of comfort as a player if you know your manager has your back. And I think that's the biggest thing. Managers that always have your back, players always want to play for those guys. Even guys on other teams, they notice those kind of things, so it's always like, people that go into free agency I know they take those things into consideration at times."

> *Mainly, just in sticking up for their guys and kind of believing in their guys. Showing confidence in you and putting you out there, letting you know, 'Hey, you're my guy. You're gonna be out there no matter what.' That's huge for a player, just knowing the manager kinda has his back and he has his support.*
>
> **Will Rhymes, infielder, Tampa Bay Rays**

Texas Rangers manager, Ron Washington, is pretty passionate about this topic. He views this as part of his duty as a manager. Washington explained it this way, "My job is to keep you free, my job is to keep you producing; and even when you're not producing, that's when I'm with you the most. There was a time there when one of my pitchers, twice, went 1 ⅔[6] innings and the media wanted me to beat him up. I said, think about it, put yourself in his position. Would you want to get beat up after you went out there and stunk up the place like that? What you need right now is love, hugs, and kisses. I'm going to tell you the right and the wrong in what happened, but I'm not going to beat you down with it because the worst person right now in that situation, is you. I look at you for what you have that's good, not at what happens to you that's bad. In this business, there's a lot happen to us that's bad, and when you sink low, that's when you need me the most, and I got your back. And what that does, that helps you to recover. As a player, the last thing I wanted to do is look over my shoulder wondering what's gonna happen. As a player, I always wanted the manager to be up-front with me, whether it hurt me or not. I wanted to know where I stand. I didn't want any surprises, because you're gonna make me better. You really are gonna make me better by telling me what's wrong with me. You're not gonna make me better by behind my back talking about it. You're gonna make me better by telling me point blank what's wrong with me, now. It's up to me to do something about it. If I don't do anything about it, I gotta carry that myself."

I've had a couple of managers where they've been put in pretty tough situations. The way they handle themselves, it would have been real easy to roll over on people, and throw other people under the bus. But, they jumped on the grenade, if you will, and they took full responsibility for it. That goes a long way for a player.
Ryan Doumit, catcher, Minnesota Twins

---

[6] As a baseball game is 9 innings, a starting pitcher who only pitches 1 ⅔ innings before being removed from the game did not have a good outing.

Overall, remember that your behavior, more than your words, will demonstrate to others whether or not you truly have their back. There will be times when tough situations call for difficult decisions and you can still demonstrate this quality by sharing a challenging message directly and honestly. If you can always strive to place your team in the best position for success and worry less about yourself, you will find that you can accomplish great things and you might even find that they will have your back too.

Be a Player's Manager

We often hear it stated that someone is a "Players' Manager" – but what exactly does that mean? It seems to be a combination of knowing your people, building relationships, supporting your people, and even knowing your game. In other words, being a players' manager encompasses many of the import *Bases of Leadership*. More often than not, players' managers tend to be the ones who have walked in the shoes of their players, generally they are former players. This isn't a requirement however, as familiarity with the game and empathy for what the game entails can be gained in other ways. Don Mattingly spoke with us about the benefits that do come from having played Major League Baseball, "I think playing, in general, helps you. I think because I've experienced a lot, I had to work my way through the minor leagues. I have an understanding of the guy that has to battle and battle. Also, being where I was one of the best players. With our guys that do really well, I've been through it, and then what comes with that. What are the pitfalls of that? What are the demands on their time and how that runs into your game? Demands of family, what's going on with kids, and travel, and what's going on with guy's families, how that demand works into your game. I try to see all those things. So, in general, just having an understanding of what's going on with those guys, try to at least, and be fair to everybody."

Players' managers tend to identify with their players and ensure that views and concerns of the players are heard at higher levels of the organization. Being a players' manager almost always aligns quite well with the concept of 'having their back'. Overall, demonstrating support to their players seems to be what makes a manager a players' manager. BJ Upton, outfielder on the Tampa Bay Rays, talked about how his manager, Joe Maddon, motivates him, "Joe's attitude alone motivates us enough. He's a player's manager. He lets you do what you need to do to get ready to play, and all he asks from you every night is just come out and play hard." That's exactly how Don Mattingly approaches his leadership because he truly understands, "I've played the game, I know you're gonna struggle at times, the game's not easy." Being a player's manager often requires putting the interests of others ahead of your own. Tom Boswell, columnist for the Washington Post, has covered baseball for many years and has a deep understanding of the philosophy of Washington National's manager, Davey Johnson. In our interview with Boswell, he noted that, "Davey's the extreme player's manager, and often that means that you have to have your players back against everybody; the media, the general manager, the owner, the fan base. And you have to sometimes conspicuously put the players' interests ahead of your own interests."

A player's manager, he could give a damn if he gets fired, he doesn't care. He's gonna do what he's gonna do because that's how he knows the best way to manage a game.

Brad Lidge, pitcher, Washington Nationals

At the heart of leadership is caring about the success of your team and being willing to give them the freedom to make decisions, to provide mentorship, and instill confidence. Ned Yost, manager of the Kansas City Royals expressed this very well, "My joy and my fun come in watching them have success, so my whole day's built around them. What can we do to make them better, what can we do to make them champions, what can we do to help them be successful? Not only in the game of baseball, but in life. Especially with young kids, I'm proud of these kids every single day when they come in and they work hard and they play hard."

Ned Yost also noted that, "You have to have a compassion and understanding about how difficult this game is to play." Ron Gardenhire, Minnesota Twins manager, discussed how he tries to keep this in his mind, especially when someone is struggling. Gardenhire said, "… you try to look at it from the players' side and work your way from there. When you forget that, it gets a little tough, you forget how hard the game is." Compassion, empathy, and understanding from managers do not go unnoticed by the players either. Michael Taylor of the Oakland A's identified his best managers as being those who remember and can empathize, those who might say, "you know what, I remember back when I played, I remember what it was like to go through a slump. I remember what it was like to doubt myself; I remember what it's like when I was riding high."

Sean Burroughs, infielder with the Twins, said he was fortunate that he has been able to play for many great managers during his career. Sean specifically mentioned Kirk Gibson, Joe Maddon, Bruce Bochy, and Ron Gardenhire and said, "They kind of want to be your friend. You know, you respect them and you play hard for them, you don't take anything for granted but you know they're always backing you, they want to see you do good, they want you to go out there and help the team. It's about winning. They want you to go out there, be successful, do things right and they're always there to help because they want you to, in the long run, be productive for the team and help the team win the ballgame." In other words, these managers build relationships and demonstrate support on a daily basis. They lead by example and are thus well respected by their players, their peers, and their organization.

Being a players' manager is easy to imagine in a clubhouse, but how can we instill this philosophy in our organizations? What do we need to do to instill a sense of support and a confidence to take chances with our teams? Simply speaking, a players' manager is one who reinforces the message that they know the most important resource in the organization is its people, and they will do whatever it takes to make sure that this resource is valued, cared for, and supported in attitude as well as action.

Instilling Confidence

Supportive leaders instill confidence in their followers, an important aspect of leadership. As leaders, you inspire through your passion but also need to encourage your people so that they believe that they can achieve, as this in turn will raise performance levels. Mike Aviles, infielder with the Boston Red Sox, stated that, "It makes it easier to go out and perform when you're comfortable and feel like the manager is confident in you and your abilities." John Farrell, Blue Jays manager, understands this very well, "I think anytime that you can show that confidence in a player and they know that you've got their back, those are the rewarding moments." Brandon Guyer, outfielder with the Tampa Bay Rays, talked about how important it is to him that his manager builds his confidence, "sometimes if I'm struggling, they'll pull me aside and sometimes just boost my confidence and tell me 'nothing's wrong, everything's gonna be alright, we love the way you play, and just keep doing what you're doing.' Little things like that can help boost your confidence."

I had to look at myself and I had to change my approach. [My approach] became more of a put my arm around him, and try to instill some confidence. There's a belief, not that I'm looking to be liked, but you build that trust, you build an environment that they can be comfortable in, and I think ultimately a comfortable player is probably a productive one.

John Farrell, manager, Toronto Blue Jays

Great leaders are the catalyst for outstanding performance. They often make the difference in whether someone is mediocre, good, or an all-star. Leading is a balancing act and you must be aware of when to push and when to give. At your core, you must believe that people desire to be great and want to succeed. With that as your starting point, it is much easier to look for the opportunity in each person versus focusing on what may have gone wrong today. That doesn't mean that you don't have firm expectations for a hard day's work and the mindset of a strong work ethic with your team. Again, there has to be give and take to achieve greatness. Don Mattingly believes in this approach to leading his team. "These guys don't come here and want to mess up, they don't want to come here and get beat. I know they want to do well. And so that's what my job is really - to keep this thing directed in that way. And when guys are going through things, if they're not working, it's a different area. Then they gotta be, you gotta let them know, 'hey, you're not doing well.' And I understand the part that you struggle, but I don't understand struggling if you don't work on it, if you don't put in time to get better. And so there's two sides to that coin: you've got to be understanding with guys and patient with guys as long as they're giving you their best effort and their getting ready to play. I have an understanding of all that."

Guys are gonna make mistakes, you know that. Guys are gonna strike out in a situation, and I know that. But give me the effort, run to first base, break up a double play, know where to throw the ball, have that killer instinct when you go out there. I don't like to be embarrassed on the baseball field.

Don Baylor, coach, Arizona Diamondbacks

This mantra of Mattingly and other big league managers is one which can be applied throughout organizations, not just ones aiming for the World Series. We have to assume that the people in our workplace want to be successful and are trying their best to do so. If, after being shown through actions and attitude that this isn't the case, then a change in our leadership might be warranted. This attitude lends itself towards a focus on support and development as opposed to one of evaluation and discipline. Certainly managers need to discipline their people at times and they need to consistently evaluate performance so that they know who to assign work to, promote, or even 'bench', but with the belief that our people want to succeed and an attitude focused on development, improved loyalty and a desire to perform and serve will follow. There are many ways that leaders can instill confidence in their team and we must continue to look for those opportunities to build up versus tear down people. Confident employees are more apt to try new things, be innovative, stay engaged, and perform at higher levels.

Become a Supportive Leader

We've discussed many of the benefits of becoming a supportive leader but what are some things that you can start doing today to help you achieve this goal? First, it's been stated a few times but bears repeating – you must know your values so that you can place logical parameters around what you will or won't stand up for with your team. This includes your values and those of your organization because, as a leader, we must be in sync with both. Next, carefully assess any possible risks. We cannot support or defend blindly so we need to know our people, be attuned to what is happening in our environment, and ensure we truly understand the situation. This will help to assess any possible risks as well as how to mitigate them, if necessary.

They know when you need a pat on the back or when you need a kick in the butt, they know the right spots to do it in. I've had managers come in after a bad loss and you're expecting to just get reamed and everything, flipping tables, the whole nine. But the exact opposite [has happened], and guys feed off it. Build confidence and lead by example.

Chris Snyder, catcher, Houston Astros

Contingency plans are great to have in these situations. As a leader, you probably know several situations that could go wrong in your environment based on your past experience, knowing your business, understanding your organization, and through the established relationships with your team members. It is helpful to have contingency plans in your mind for how you might react in certain situations. This will never be a complete list but it could be broken into categories and types of issues. By thinking through this in advance, even new situations are easier to assess and place into a most likely scenario for next steps.

When defending someone, it is important that you maintain positive working relationships with all concerned. This requires diplomacy and use of empathy to achieve the outcome you most desire. Depending on the situation, you may need to offer a resolution or even share what steps you have already taken to resolve the conflict or performance matter. It is critical to your reputation that you treat all members of your team the same and that you afford a similar support system to each of them. Situations such as this are very easy to be misconstrued as favoritism; therefore, a consistent approach is very important.

Once you have supported (or defended) someone publically, it is important to have follow up with the individual in private. This can lead to an excellent learning opportunity for everyone. You may discover a deficiency in training, resources, and other team members that needs to be addressed separately. It also provides a terrific platform for coaching because you have established a baseline of trust on the front-end and this makes the person being coached much more susceptible to feedback and direction. Keep a heart for leadership and truly seek to help each person become their best!

A trip to the mound...

- In what ways do I demonstrate support to my team?

- Would members of my team say I have their backs?

- Do my experiences and relationships give me a foundation to be considered a player's manager?

- What behaviors do I regularly display that help instill confidence in my team?

- How can I more effectively use my core values to create parameters for support?

Chapter 7
Communicate Effectively

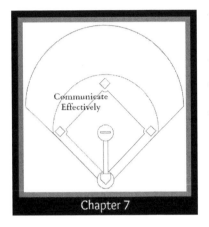

You need to know what you need to improve on and what you need to work on. If you're gonna sit there and get lip service, that's not going to help you.

Kyle Weiland, pitcher, Houston Astros

Both players and managers realize the importance of communication to their success. Players want to know what's going on, and successful managers want their players to be comfortable coming to them to find out.   This is Leadership 101, to have a successful organization, people at all levels need to understand their roles, understand their goals, and understand how they are expected to accomplish them. They also, as successful leaders understand, need to communicate to their people how their actions each day play a part in the overall success of the organization; how the utility man is important to the team, and how the 25th man on the roster plays a valuable role in the win. Your position isn't what is most important to you as a leader, what is most important is your vision and how effective you can be in communicating it and engaging others into it.

Don Mattingly, MLB All-Star first baseman and, as we've identified, current manager of the Los Angeles Dodgers, does his best to communicate with his players as much as he can so that he can "let them know where they stand and let them know what's going on."

He feels it's important "to let them know what (he's) thinking." The conversations between managers and players don't need to be long talks each day, as Darren Oliver of the Blue Jays points out, they can be short five minute conversations, just enough for the player to know that their manager is thinking about them, and is available for them. This attitude of openness and accessibility was echoed by managers and players throughout Major League Baseball and is understood by successful leaders all over, communication is key.

It is easy to throw around the word 'communication' as in its simplest form it implies that someone talks and another person listens. This however, is not all there is. George Bernard Shaw illustrated this fallacy very well when he said, "The single biggest problem in communication is the illusion that it has taken place."[17]
Communication is a process, it takes effort, and it takes leadership. To communicate most effectively with members of your team it is useful to have a relationship built on trust and respect, and have a focus on common goals. In other words, for communication to be effective the other *Bases of Leadership* that we have discussed already need to be in place.

> *...an open line of communication and dialogue. Whether it's good or bad, you're always able to go to that man, your manager, for anything. I think that's important.*
>
> **Carl Pavano, pitcher, Minnesota Twins**

How do We do It?

What are some of the ways that you communicate with others in your workplace? Do you purposefully walk to them to let them know you are interested in what they are working on or how they are doing as manager John Farrell does during batting practice when he walks the 300 feet to visit with his players in the outfield? Do you open your door for your people figuratively letting them know that you are available whenever they need you as Bob Melvin of the A's does to let his players know their role for an upcoming series and *why* they are or aren't in the lineup? Do you have a door on your office that remains open whenever possible like Minnesota Twins manager Ron Gardenhire so that your employees know that they are welcome to come in whenever they need? Players, as Sean Burroughs told us and other players on the Twins roster reiterated, know that they "can go in and talk to [Gardenhire] about anything, anytime." These practices, the ways that we show our people that we are available, have a major impact on the way we are viewed by them and others, and have a major impact on how successful we are in guiding our team to achieve success, however that success is gauged.

One point to remember, and something which was pointed out to us by Indians manager, Manny Acta, was that even though the 'door is always open' not all players are always comfortable coming in, not many "like to come to the manager's office." This is certainly not indicative of all organizations, but in the time we spent in Major League clubhouses we did notice that the manager's office is a place that not many players ventured unless invited. Players, when they get to the ballpark (way before game time as we've discussed), have a routine and in many ways manage themselves. They know they need to work out, they know if they need to spend some time with the trainer, and they know when it's time to take BP or do some fielding. Communication of these things isn't necessary, and thus unless there is an issue or something which needs clarification, they don't generally need an audience with their manager. In the workplace many times, this is the same; we know our jobs and have our goals, so why is it that communication is so important? The simple answer is that communication serves a few purposes; information, support, and inspiration. No matter what position we are in, these three, at different levels, are important. A player, just as an employee or volunteer in any organization, wants to feel comfortable sharing the issues they may have and they want to feel confident that their manager is paying attention to them and their needs.

If a manager is very open and receptive and able to talk, it makes you play a little better. You know you can talk some things out, figure out a better solution. If I feel one way and the manager feels another way and we talk about it and we come to a compromise, or if I understand where he's coming from, you can do what you need to do to be the player he wants.
Scott Atchison, pitcher, Boston Red Sox

A term that is used often in management trainings is that of the 'open door policy'. This policy, in theory, is great, if an employee has a problem; their manager is there for them *whenever* they would like. Well, in practice this is not quite as pretty, as managers, both inside and outside of the Game, have their own work to do! It's for this reason that a modified open door policy is one which can be more effective and palatable for managers. In this proposed policy managers would be available anytime one of their people needs support or guidance for something that is critical, but for things which aren't critical there are hours which are set aside each day for players or employees to come in and discuss whatever they want. With this type of policy managers are available for their people whenever needed for something vital and which requires immediate attention, available for anything their people need during a set time each day, and otherwise, they have time to get their own work done...it's a win/win! The manager gets work done and the people, players or employees, know that their manager is there for them when needed, something that players like

Brad Ziegler, pitcher for the Arizona Diamondbacks, and others, find to be important for their success. Ziegler expressed to us how much it means to him that his manager Kirk Gibson wants to make sure that he's comfortable "so that when [he goes] out on the mound, it's smooth sailing." Communicating with others effectively, sharing information and establishing a relationship serves to benefit not only the individual but also the organization and its goals. No matter what industry we are in, if we are secure that our manager wants to hear from us and values us we are more apt to give to the organization our commitment, loyalty, satisfaction, and superior performance...and that equates to wins for the team!

Vision - Having it, Communicating it, and Living it

Leadership guru, Warren Bennis, has said that part of being a good leader is having a vision that is well communicated. This simple statement has large implications both inside and outside of baseball. Let's imagine for a moment a manager who has his eyes on the prize, winning the World Series. Now let's imagine that this manager is a great strategist and knows the X's and O's of the game (something which as we discussed in Chapter 8 is an important *Base of Leadership*). Finally let's imagine that this manager doesn't connect with his team, doesn't know how to capitalize on their strengths and minimize their shortcomings, and doesn't know how to communicate to his players their role, their importance, and the value they add to the mix. This manager, as 'baseball' smart as he may be, is not going to hold that coveted trophy because of his inability to communicate to his team the vision he has for not only the team but for each player individually. Good managers like John Farrell understand the importance of communicating a vision. They not only, as Farrell told us, "put a goal out there that's realistic, but at the same time, give them [the players] thoughts on how we're to go about their work and the way we play the game." Good managers, as Farrell continued, "realize that in order for their vision to be fulfilled they need to engage and empower each member of their team."

I've always respected the person that was coaching me and felt like that every coach I have is trying to make me better. I appreciate the kind words and also respect the criticism because I feel like they're in a position to try to make you better and I look at it from that point of view.

Jamey Carroll, pitcher, Minnesota Twins

Having a vision that is well communicated is not just about communicating the vision for the team, but also about using the expertise and know-how that have helped the manager attain his (or her) position to help their people get not only where they want to go, but where they need to go. Red Sox pitcher, Andrew Bailey, stressed to us that he, along with many of his counterparts throughout the league, always want to play and contribute their all to the team. Sometimes, as is also the case outside of baseball, players and employees don't always see their limitations, and it is then up to the manager, as Bailey told us, "to sometimes override [them] and do what's right." Players throughout the league communicated to us that if they trust their manager they may not always be happy with his decision, but they will respect it and accept it. With trust in our managers and a well communicated vision we are more apt to accept our roles and work with our managers to succeed at them.

Tell Them How It Is

Bob Melvin shared with us that he tries his best to make sure that each member of his team understands their role and sees the value in it. As manager of the A's, Melvin has been quite successful leaning heavily on open communication as a tool in his leadership toolkit. When we spoke with Melvin prior to the 2012 season he explained that upon taking over as manager of his team he explained to his players that he would keep their personal goals and needs in mind, but they needed to try to see things from his perspective as well. Melvin shared with us that he feels that he has a good understanding of the need and manner of how to communicate with his back up players since he spent his playing career in that role. He explained that to be successful he needs his players to all be engaged and one of the ways he does this is by giving his backup players something to look forward to. He explained that for a backup player who comes to the park expecting to play that not seeing his name on the lineup card can be demoralizing, and for that reason he is as clear as possible about under what circumstances his players will see action. Melvin explained, "I always let them know a couple days ahead of time, 'that's your guy, that's your guy. In two days, you're starting against that guy' so they can start their process and get, go do some video. I mean this is like a football game for these guys because 'not only do I get to play, and do I know I'm going to play in a couple of days, this is a guy I've had success against!' Now he's really looking forward to something. I tell them, 'this is your role, this is what's expected.' If there's a particular game where I have a guy on the bench who has a real good matchup against a reliever, I'll make sure I go over there and tell him, 'if that guy even moves down there, you get up and get ready because that's your guy.' And he'll know 'I've got some hits off this guy.'"

Melvin's leadership certainly had a positive impact on the A's, as in the two full seasons that he has been manager the team has a record of 190 wins and 134 losses and has made it to the divisional series both years. The impact that sharing information and rationale with those who are impacted should not be understated. When Melvin, as discussed above, shares with his players how and why they will be playing, they may not always be happy but they will respect and understand the reasoning. Tom Boswell, Washington Post columnist and author, shared with us a story about how a manager he covered quite extensively, Davey Johnson, communicated with one of his players as well as the Washington press to let everyone know that the struggling player was 'his guy' and need not worry about his position being taken by another newly signed player (who was switching positions). Boswell explained to us that Johnson was very firm with the media telling them not to revisit the question again about his struggling player, and that he did this for his player's benefit so he would be confident and go play his game.

Being able to communicate with the players. That's the big issue in this generation of baseball, being able to communicate, actually really listening to them, because they have strong opinions today in the game. In my day, when the manager spoke he was like E.F. Hutton, and that was the end of it. But [the players] have strong opinions, so I think the toughest thing is listening to them. Really, after you listen to them, try to continue to guide them.

Ron Washington, manager, Texas Rangers

Tell It Like It Is

In baseball as well as in any organization, communication, directives, goals, and vision can come from various sources with many managers and organizational leaders providing us with guidance and structure. A baseball manager's job, like that of a front line manager, is to make sure that messages are delivered clearly, timely, and from the right person. John Farrell explains that his coaches on the Blue Jays play a vital role on his team, helping him to communicate direction, and helping him to develop and communicate strategy. He, along with the other managers we spoke with, also relies on his coaches to help communicate his vision and his messages. Ron Washington pointed to the fact that having a good coaching staff who can effectively communicate his message, like the one he has in Texas, "makes your job as a leader and a manager that much easier."

So what messages should a manager deliver directly and what messages should a manager rely on his coaches to deliver? John Farrell told us that he allows his coaches to handle many issues with the players, but when something major arises then he as the manager needs to be the one to communicate that to the team. Mattingly expands on this point as well saying that, "even if they don't necessarily like what I'm telling them, at least they're hearing it from me." A leader makes sure that he is in touch with his people, and they are in touch with him. As Harry Truman's famous desk sign read, "The Buck Stops Here", and leaders know that if there is a serious message to be delivered it should be delivered by the person who is ultimately making the call, and in many cases in baseball, that is with the manager. Managers need to remember that as much as they don't like messages to be 'sugarcoated', their players don't like that either. As Michael Taylor of the Oakland A's told us, he doesn't like when a manager sugar coats a situation, he'd rather a manager come out and say, "hey look, this is your role, this is where we see you now. This is what you have to do if you want to change your role. Or 'you don't really have an opportunity right now, just keep working hard and we'll see where things are down the road." Players, as employees in all walks of life, want to know that they are receiving the guidance and messages they need in order to be successful and continue to develop. They shouldn't have to guess the vision and ideas of their leaders. Their managers, as Don Mattingly told us, should "try to just be up front and open, it's fairly simple."

You communicate to them, 'hey look, you're not an everyday player.' They might not like it but they'll respect you for it. 'Here's your role, here's what I expect you to do to stay ready for your role.'

Bob Melvin, manager, Oakland A's

In some cases players do not like what they hear, and in some cases they are not given as much information as they would like. Ron Washington, manager, Texas Rangers, uses what he and others have called 'preaching' to help his players learn "the right thing". Washington acknowledged to us that sometimes players get the message quickly and other times it takes them a little while, but with that he will continue to preach his message, as he knows that what he is saying will help them and help the team. Washington went on to say, "If you don't get the message, it won't be because the message wasn't valid. It will only be because you just couldn't absorb it. You can't save everybody, but you can try to help everybody."

This is not something which is specific to Major League Baseball as quite often employees are not given the full picture of their organization's strategy. This is something which can be quite discouraging and upsetting to an employee or a player, not having confidence that their manager has their best interests at heart. Relief pitcher Craig Breslow has played for some managers who are more forthcoming than others as far as why or why not they use certain players in given situations, and he made the point to us that as much as he would like to know his manager's rationale, this isn't always his right to know, " I have every right to ask the manager. But I also at times am okay with the fact that he's the guy that makes the decisions and there's a reason that he's leading the team. But again this kind of falls into that trust thing." With trust, managers do not always need to explain every detail.

To Meet or Not to Meet

Meetings can have a negative connotation as people often consider them a time waster, and even unproductive. This view is one shared by players in the Major Leagues as well as employees throughout various industries. Players at the Major League level know what they need to do, just as most employees know what they need to do on a day to day basis, so, as Edwin Jackson of the Washington Nationals told us, "the great managers, they let the team go out and play and do what they're here to do."

Certainly meetings can serve an important purpose if used for the right reasons and at the right times. Often information needs to be shared with an entire team, some team building is in order, or an entire team is in need of a jolt. In cases like this a team meeting would be warranted. Joe Maddon, has a strong opinion on the team meeting and told us that in general he thinks they are "actually worthless." This doesn't mean that he doesn't hold meetings, it just means that he holds them infrequently, and only when needed. Maddon actually has some interesting guidelines which he follows when it comes to team meetings, he tries to only hold them on the road (so as not to 'stain' the home clubhouse with negativity, and he tries to hold them only after wins and not losses as he feels that when a team loses games the players need your support not your anger.

Team meetings are viewed by many as unnecessary and even de-motivating. If they are held too often then their impact can be diminished, and if they are not effectively providing information, goals, or development, there are better uses of a player or employee's time. This opinion is echoed by many throughout industry as well as baseball, who feel that their time could be better used outside of meetings than sitting in them.

When designing a meeting it is important to have an agenda of items that needs to be covered, take-a-way goals for each person who is in the meeting (if they don't have something to do when they leave why were they there?), and some inspiration by the leader or the manager, as to how to take their jobs to the next level. A manager should have a firm understanding prior to the meeting of the 'must accomplish', 'should accomplish', and 'hope to accomplish' messages, and items that he or she wants to address. Maddon, a successful manager, and one who is considered one of the best in the Game, said that he doesn't hold meetings to discuss becoming better hitters or doing better in specific situations, but that he holds meetings only when there are issues with the 'core beliefs' of the team. He understands and respects that his players know what they need to do (hit the ball, field the ball, and throw the ball), so there's no reason to meet about that, but if they aren't playing hard, as Maddon identified, then a deeper issue must be addressed.

Meetings are held if the team doesn't follow those core philosophies which make for an effective team. If we don't hustle, we don't play hard, and if there's a perception that you're not caring enough. That's what the meeting's gonna be about.

Joe Maddon, manager, Tampa Bay Rays

Meetings within MLB clubhouses are often called for a purpose, just as meetings outside of the game are often scheduled by managers for a specific purpose. The problem is that many meetings, both in and out of the game, are filled with the manager talking, feeding information, and sharing what he or she feels is most important, leading to a passive audience. A truly effective meeting should include active participants, as we have to assume that the people in the meeting, the people on your team, are all there for a reason and have something to contribute.

Manny Acta shared his philosophy, and one that meshes well with that of exemplary leadership; players and employees need to be made to feel like they are a part of a decision. Acta continued, "it doesn't mean that they're dictating [the decisions], but they feel like they're a part of it." In business this is certainly important as if we want our people to be empowered to perform and to go above and beyond, they need to be made to feel like they are valued, appreciated, and heard.

I Hear You

For many it is difficult to see things through the eyes of others. In fact, emotional intelligence, a growing field of study which includes being empathetic and aware of other's perspectives, directs people to this important leadership concept. A cornerstone of emotional intelligence is listening, being able to hear what your counterpart is saying and understand their reasoning and their intentions. Former New York Met and current hitting coach of the Seattle Mariners, Howard "HoJo" Johnson, reflected with us about his time playing with Davey Johnson, Sparky Anderson, and other managers, and about how important and meaningful it was for him that his managers would listen to him, hear his perspective, and consider his opinions. HoJo's sentiments were reiterated by many of today's players as well with one of Johnson's current players, Bryce Harper, telling us that "being able to sit down, talk, and really express yourself with what you feel like you can help the team with" is important to him and others on the club. What was implied by Harper and told to us by many players is that they value when a manager truly listens to them and goes out of his way to bring them into a conversation, share with them ideas, and talk strategy with them. Joe Maddon shared with us what he thinks is one of the most important leadership skills, the ability to listen. "I think you need to be a great listener. I think most of the time, when there is a problem with a player; they will normally answer their own questions if you're able to listen. I think too many times we have a tendency to walk over a conversation. If somebody's answering you, you're always wanting to interject what you know. If you give yourself the opportunity or the time to just listen to them, most of the time you're gonna hear something good that you're eventually going to be able to throw back at them and then thus, they're going to answer their own questions, [manage] their own problems. Listening is probably one of the most important things I do here."

"Answer their own questions," as Maddon said, if you give your players a forum to speak and you listen to what they're saying and interject some of your own knowledge to a situation, often they will answer their own questions. The art of listening truly is an art, and those people who understand and appreciate that are the best leaders. To listen we need to be active participants, we can't be anticipating our next comment or thinking about where we will be eating dinner, we need to listen, acknowledge, question, validate, and participate. A baseball player, an engineer, a marketing rep, or a human resources specialist all have something in common (along with all the other fields out there), they are in their position because they have some ability, and thus they need to be given the respect from those who they are speaking with that they have a knowledge and perspective that can be used to help solve a problem or advance a cause. With a philosophy like that of Milwaukee Brewers manager, Ron Roenicke, giving his players the freedom to say what's on their minds, leaders can draw out from their players interesting perspectives and with some validation, questioning, and direction, they can participate in their own problem solving. Asking "why" is something that long time coach Matt Sinatro says is something he has always encouraged his players to do. "There should be a reason why we're telling them something," Sinatro told us, "there's got to be a reason, and you know what, 99% of the time, when they question you, and when you give them a good reason, they're fine." We need to always remember that we are, as Peter Drucker coined us, *knowledge workers*, who have much to contribute to our organizations, so, as leaders and coaches told us, it makes sense to listen.

If they have something to say to you, you listen, you talk about it, and you see what's best...

Ricky Romero, pitcher, Toronto Blue Jays

Consistency is Key

Being a Major League Baseball manager in itself lends credibility to what is being said, just as becoming the CEO of a company gives the CEO's words credibility. That said, it is very easy to lose credibility when trust in the person who is delivering the message is diminished, and very easy to lose credibility when the message that is being delivered is different each time the manager speaks. This somewhat simple, but poignant point, is an important one. A manager needs to be consistent in the message he is delivering and in the manner in which it is being delivered. Joe Maddon shared with us that his demeanor and style haven't changed since he began his career as a manager. When his teams were losing he was criticized for not being tough enough, but when they were winning, the criticism goes away. When communicating Maddon, as well as other managers, deliver a consistent message, they want their players to develop their strengths and look to their coaches to help them to excel. Managers outside of baseball also should focus their message on development and on working towards a common goal. In baseball it is the coveted World Series trophy, as we've mentioned before, and every organization needs to help their people realize what trophy they should strive to achieve. The ways in which people work to get to the goal may be different but the message must remain the same, develop, work hard, and help the team, help the organization to reach their goals.

A trip to the mound...

- Is my vision being communicated effectively?

- Does my team know how to achieve success individually and collectively?

- Are members of my team comfortable coming to me when needed? What can I do to encourage this?

- Do I listen to the concerns of my team and acknowledge their contributions?

- Am I consistent with my message?

Part Three

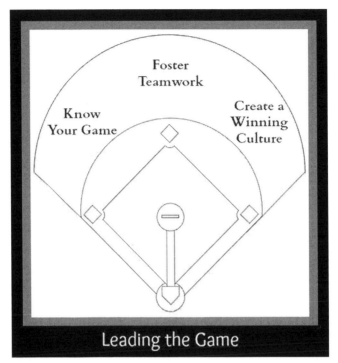

Leading the Game

Completing our blueprint of the baseball diamond, we finish in the outfield. This is the largest area of the field, can feel safe due to the high walls, but at the same time, dangerous because of the wide open sky. This is similar to the walls of our business, the opportunity for expansion and innovation, and also, the thrill of competition with the desire to succeed – all components of *Leading the Game*. First up, the left fielder who, like leaders, must *Know his Game* and be ready for anything. The centerfielder covers the most expansive area and truly leads the outfield requiring expert us of the next *Base – Fostering Teamwork*. The final position, the right fielder, often has an opportunity to make the winning catch to end the game. Bringing it all together, we reach our final *Base – Create a Winning Culture*. Success is measured by goals and your ultimate destination. The *Bases of Major League Leadership* will guide us to reach our destination.

After seven chapters of discussing the ways managers lead themselves and lead others so that they can best present their vision and inspire others to follow it, commit to it, and adopt it, we now get to the final *Bases of Leadership*, those related to the game itself. In this final component of *Major League Leadership* we will delve into what many inside the game call the "X's and O's", the strategy, the team, and the way day by day and game time decisions are made.

Getting to know our 'game,' whether we are truly discussing a game such as baseball or referring to the 'game' we do each day, our work or business, encompasses many of the same components, we need to understand the ins and outs of our organization and understand the ways to be successful. One of the ways to be successful in all we do is by understanding that we are not alone. We have coaches, we have assistants, we have peers, and we have project teams...to be most successful we need to learn how to use all the pieces of our team in unison and capitalize on their strengths.

As a manager you rely on your coaching staff and you rely on your players. I always tell these players; you know 'I'm out here to help you because when I help you that means job security.' When they're playing good baseball and we're getting it done, that's job security.

Ron Gardenhire, manager, Minnesota Twins

Our second *Base of Leadership* in this Part of the book is *Foster Teamwork*. Once we understand how to lead ourselves, the importance of getting to know our players, the significance of developing relationships, and the benefit of supporting our people and 'having their back', we then work on building our team and capitalizing on all the individual strengths that our players have. In baseball we need to understand that we can't play every position ourselves, and in business we need to understand that if we try we will minimize our team and the outcome will not be as powerful as if we all worked together. One common denominator when discussing team dynamics is that to be most effective on a team we need to take pride in the team that we are a part of, and hopefully, in the organization as well. Developing and cultivating this pride is done partially through the actions of the manager who is the voice of the organization to his team. The manager must create a culture of pride amongst his players, both for the team and for the organization they are playing for, and one way to do this is by representing the team in a positive manner. As Bob Melvin told us, "when you have pride in leadership and you believe in your leader, you come to work with a smile on your face, and take pride in playing for [your] organization."

> *They are doing a lot of instruction with the younger guys and the way that we like to do things around here. We [veterans] know what they expect from us. There's not a whole lot of teaching with the guys that have been around, it's just, 'alright, this is how we did it last year. We need to try and do this a little bit better. But you guys know what you're doing.'*
>
> **Ryan Voglesong, pitcher, San Francisco Giants**

The managers we spoke with all have different styles of how to engage their teams and communicate these messages. The styles varied from that of former New York Mets manager Bud Harrelson's "loosey goosey" approach, to Don Baylor's focus on education and strategy, and to Rays manager, Joe Maddon's belief that, "there's a lot of discipline involved by giving freedom." Each style is different and each will be most effective with certain types of players and under certain situations. It's up to the manager and the front office to know which manager is the best fit at a given time and with a certain roster of players. This leads us to our final *Base of Leadership*, destination - *Creating* a *Winning Culture*. A culture is something which is created over time and often has some bumps in the road with people being added to the team and people leaving who don't fit the vision. Ron Washington, Texas Rangers manager, told us that he was the proudest in 2009, "I had to change the culture around here, how you think, how you act, and how you go about your business. Because around here in Texas it was one way, and it wasn't conducive to being successful. The only way you can be successful is everybody that's involved has to be a part of what's trying to get done." In order for a team in baseball or a team in any organization to be successful its players need to believe they can be successful. Although teams may not believe in Spring Training that they can make it to the World Series, it is up to the manager to help them focus on achieving one win at a time, on focusing on the small wins, and eventually the 'big' win will seem more achievable. It's up to the manager to use our final *base*, and create a winning culture in his clubhouse.

Chapter 8
Know your Game

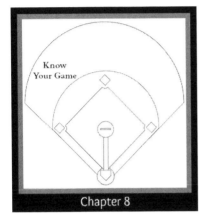

You want somebody that has an intelligent baseball mind; somebody that thinks the game, somebody you feel like is going to be one step ahead of the guy in the other dugout.

Gerry Hunsicker, Sr. Vice President,
Tampa Bay Rays

"Knowledge is Power", the phrase attributed to Sir Francis Bacon in the 16th Century certainly holds true in the game of baseball as well as the game of life! As leaders, amongst other things, we need to have a strong knowledge of our 'game.' We need to provide the tools for success to those around us and be a resource to the players we are responsible for leading. To do this, we need to have a firm grasp on those things which are important to our people. Along with the other *Bases of Leadership* we discussed, the X's and O's, as they are referred to by many in baseball, the strategy and gameplay we employ in all our activities, are also vital for organizational and personal success. A "knowledge of the game always helps" was said in a matter of fact way by Ron Gardenhire as he pointed to the importance that he attributes to remembering 'what it was like to be a player.'

The experiences he had as a backup catcher during his playing days helped shape the leadership philosophy of A's manager, Bob Melvin. Melvin shared that feelings of uncertainty are often felt by backup players, not knowing when they would be coming to bat or playing the field next. He used these examples to illustrate why he maintains open communication with his players and shares with them the plans he has for his starting and bench players for each game, each series, and even for the season. Ned Yost, manager of the Kansas City Royals, echoed similar sentiments about the need to keep his players informed of his strategy so that confusion would be kept at a minimum and focus maintained. "When our players walk in, it doesn't matter what time they walk in, they know exactly what they're doing, I think that's very important. Confusion is something that we want to totally eliminate because in order to become a champion, you have to be focused."

In this chapter we will look at the importance of knowing your game as a leader. First, you must ensure you have the fundamental "hard skills" necessary to lead effectively. Second, it is important that you gain the necessary expertise within your organization and industry so you can have the deeper knowledge needed for decision-making. Third, it is vital to understand that leadership is about performance, and that discipline and consistency are typically required to establish appropriate expectations. Leadership is not without challenges, and we must embrace them in order to become a true agent of change. When we view challenges as opportunities we are more apt to successfully navigate them. Finally, by managing the game, by executing strategy, we become a results-oriented leader.

Fundamentals Build the Foundation

Up to this point, we have discussed mostly what are termed as "soft skills." These are more about who a leader is and include such things as passion, values, character, people skills, and emotional intelligence. These soft skills tend to be what separates good leaders from great ones because it defines how things get done. But what a leader does day to day as far as planning, strategizing, and managing, is also important, this is where the "hard skills" come into play. These skills may be simply defined as occupational skills or what you must be able to do in order to execute tangible job elements. Industry differences aside, being a leader has many hard skills such as critical thinking, aptitude for decision making, capability to synthesize data, and ability to prioritize and define goals. These are the things which when executed effectively show that the leader truly 'knows the game'.

Gibby [Kirk Gibson] goes about it the same way that I went about it. Same way. Don't leave any stones unturned. We gotta work on this, we gotta work on that, every day. Sliding practice, hit the cutoff man, all the things that he learned from Sparky [Anderson]. Same thing he learned from Earl [Weaver].

Don Baylor, hitting coach, Arizona Diamondbacks

During our time with the members of Major League Baseball, it was very evident that players, managers, and executives had a strong expectation that leaders needed to be proficient in the hard skills or fundamentals of the game. Although they each recognized the importance of the soft skills, they made it clear that the tangible job elements were the foundation upon which a manager's success was built. Ron Gardenhire talked about how he really likes to find ways to make players better, and this comes from having fundamental knowledge of the game. He shared, "I like to be able to help players out, try to make them better. So to see them go out there and you work on something and then it comes forth in the game, the same situation and they get a base hit, and telling them learn to drive the ball the other way, this is what they're trying to do and they get that hit, you feel good about it. I mean, that's the satisfaction you get as a manager." And that's one of the greatest feelings that a leader can have – knowing that you have helped someone in a tangible way and now you are seeing them succeed. This is a very rewarding side of leadership and it comes through having a great sense of the hard skills.

Davey's [Johnson] got a way of demonstrating how you drop your top hand on the ball in the middle of the swing, anyway, he worked with [Ian] Desmond on that. He's extremely good at getting a team to relax, he's good at getting a team to play intelligently.

Tom Boswell, columnist, Washington Post

Fundamentals go a long way. Don Baylor had a great career as a player and also won National League Manager of the Year in 1995 with the Colorado Rockies. He later became the Hitting Coach for the Atlanta Braves and subsequently Arizona Diamondbacks. Baylor shared with us a great story about a legendary player, Chipper Jones, "It was '99 when I went over there. I told him, I said 'You know, managing against you, I would love to switch around and let you hit left, let you hit right handed, because you're a singles guy.' So I said, 'What we're gonna do while I'm here is you're gonna become a better right handed hitter like you were before.' Because he spent so much time on the left side, left side. So we go to a cage, just about every day that whole year. I think he hit like 20 homers from the right side, ended up with 45. Won his MVP over there. But here's a guy that was already successful, bought into it, and most good guys that are, do that, they gotta be." That's a great example of how superior fundamental skills can have a winning effect on an already outstanding player. Imagine if every leader took the time to share their knowledge and skills in this manner with their team. A common mistake that managers make is that they let their top performers "continue what they're doing" since they are successful already, and focus their time on the new members of their team or the underperformers. As much as the underperformers need to be developed and the new team members need to learn, the manager is in a position to help everyone, and Don Baylor's example above shows exactly why. Managers outside of the game could benefit from spending time developing all their players at all levels.

Tom Boswell has spent his career as a columnist for the Washington Post. He has also authored several books on baseball including, "Game Day," "The Heart of the Order" "Strokes of Genius," "Why Time Begins on Opening Day" and "How Life Imitates the World Series." With this experience comes many years of observing and analyzing leaders in the sports industry and spending quite a bit of time with Washington Nationals manager, Davey Johnson. Boswell shared some insights with us including how Johnson's fundamental baseball skills have helped him to be successful in the game, "He goes out and teaches the second baseman how to turn the double play the way he did when he won his Gold Gloves. Or he gives hitting instruction. It was easier for him 20 years ago [earlier in his managerial career] because people knew he had been an all-star 3 or 4 times and won the Gold Glove 3 or 4 times. They knew the story about how he, late in his career he ended up in Atlanta, the same team as Hank Aaron, and Hank Aaron taught him a special move and the swing that gave him more power, and all of a sudden Davey, who'd only hit 10 or 15 home runs, hit 43 home runs in one year in Atlanta and tied Roger Hornsby's all time record for the most home runs ever hit by a second baseman. Everybody was just like 'That's not possible! You can't wake up 10 years into your career and hit 43 home runs!'"

But it is possible, and Davey Johnson was able to use his fundamental skills to become an outstanding Major League Baseball player and in turn outstanding MLB Manager. Johnson was the first National League Manager to win at least 90 games in each of his first five seasons. He led the New York Mets to win the 1986 World Series Championship and was inducted into their Hall of Fame in 2010. Most recently, he led the

Washington Nationals to their first division title as the Nationals[7] and won National League Manager of the Year in 2012. Overall, Johnson's balance of soft skills and hard skills gave him a lifetime managing winning percentage of .562. A lesson we can all learn from Davey Johnson, find a way to balance the fundamental occupational skills with the behavioral soft skills.

Expertise is Essential

Many qualities are required to be an effective leader, but a focus on expertise seems to be regaining importance over the last several years. Being an expert in your field was previously one of the primary methods of being promoted; however, organizations discovered that experience alone did not necessarily translate into being an effective manager or leader. The prior trend away from this area led to many disconnects in the workplace and often an inability to truly understand the business at a level that enabled great decision making. Leadership skills combined with deep expertise is a winning combination for success. Organizations run by leaders who have worked their way up in the company or the industry are successful, and household names such as: Starbucks, UPS, Apple, IBM, and Oracle fit this model. This combination holds true as well in Major League Baseball.

Ted Simmons was a guy that I played with, Teddy taught me how to play the game. He taught me how to look deeper than just playing the game; he taught me how to study the game.

Ned Yost, manager, Kansas City Royals

---

[7] The Washington Nationals came into existence in 2004 when the Montreal Expos moved from Montreal to Washington D.C

We discussed previously how having experience in the role helps a leader become more empathetic with their team and how some of the great leaders in Major League Baseball started out as players and are now beloved and respected as players' managers. This all relates to the need for expertise. When we asked Davey Johnson about what he thinks makes an effective manager in the major leagues, he responded, "I look at qualifications, the qualifications to being a big league manager...well, number one is managing in the minor leagues, managing - ideally, managing talent that is in your organization. If you're looking at a blueprint to find who would be the best leader, manager, whatever you want to call him, skipper to me, it would be managing in the system, being a good evaluator of talent, and seeing how your concept of leadership sets with the players."

This expectation comes from the players' view point as well. Gio Gonzalez, a pitcher for Johnson on the Washington Nationals talked about the importance of expertise. He said, "We're not all going to have answers, and that's what they [managers] are there for. It's always the veteran guys or the coaches or guys who've had years of experience that know what they're saying, know what they're doing." As Gonzalez stated, the leader is expected to have the answers; to know how to guide everyone each day. Chris Snyder discussed how this level of expertise earns his respect as a catcher on the Houston Astros. He said. "You don't wake up one day and say, 'Hey, I'm gonna try to be a big league manager tomorrow.' They know the game, they've studied the game, and they've been in battles. Their credentials show that they deserve to be there. So with that said, they're already starting ahead, there's already that earned respect."

It really should be no different in the corporate world, our employees have the expectation that we are experts in our field, someone they can turn to for advice and coaching, and someone they can respect. These attributes give a leader expert power; people believe you can help them become successful. This type of power is much more lasting and authentic than positional power as people *want* to follow leaders with expertise since they can see the mutual benefit that can be achieved. When someone follows a leader based on their position they will do enough to keep their job, when they follow someone for their expertise they will go above and beyond as they know they will learn from and generate respect from that person. Jamey Carroll, when he was with the Minnesota Twins, told us that, "getting a chance to play for somebody like Frank Robinson, who played this game for a long time, to me, that's respect factor number one. When he talked, you listened." There are limits to expertise and it is important that we surround ourselves with people who are strong in areas where we may be deficient. This is where our coaching staff (supervisors and other managers) can truly bring balance and perspective. There are many opportunities for team members to share their expertise and shine in the workplace.

It helps if you have validity as a player. Everybody, 99% of the managers at some point, played. That certainly helps. For me, I was a coach before I was a manager.

**Bud Harrelson, former manager,
New York Mets**

Discipline Establishes Expectations

Great leaders desire to achieve results and are typically results and performance driven. To be successful in this goal requires clear expectations of each member of the team and that there is appropriate motivation as well as discipline to ensure those expectations and personal commitments are met. It's all about having a performance-driven mindset. When it comes to achieving high levels of performance, it takes discipline, consistency, and the ability to customize your approach to fit the needs of each team member. Terry Ryan, GM, Minnesota Twins, shared his thoughts on what it takes to be a Major League Baseball Manager: "He's got to have discipline; he's got to have rules and follow them."

When talking about discipline and tough love, Ron Washington shared this story from his playing days, "My very first manager in rookie ball, I had him out of high school, first time I've ever left my city of New Orleans, he was a tough character, very tough character, but he loved us. And I could see the love, but I could also see him trying to be tough, and I'm saying to myself, 'He's not as tough as he pretended to be,' but I understood what he was doing. His name was Buzzy Keller, my very first manager. And then my second manager I had, his name was Steve Boros, the Lord bless his soul, he's passed away. I was a catcher and I used to drop balls. So all of a sudden he just came to me and challenged me and said, 'For every ball you drop, you owe me a dollar, and for every game you get through where you don't drop a ball, I owe you a dollar.' Say whoa, something's wrong with this picture. I got to go behind the dish nine innings and if I make it through a game without dropping a ball you giving me a dollar. But for every ball I drop, I got to pay you? But that challenge right there made me focus; made me understand what focus was. See what I'm saying? And at that time a dollar was a dollar. So I couldn't afford to be giving him four or five dollars every night. And it got the point where I went through games where I never dropped it. And I was in his pocket. But what he taught me by doing that as a young man at 18 years old is how to focus."

I'm the guy where I can use a kick in the butt more than a pat on the back. I've fed off that and I do well with that.
Chris Snyder, catcher, Houston Astros

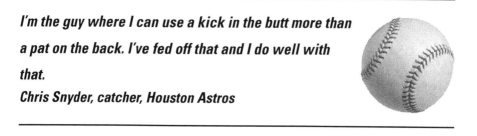

Now, I doubt we can get away with fining employees in the workplace today but the idea can certainly be duplicated. What Steve Boros did for a young Ron Washington was to measure and track his performance. What we keep track of and talk about is remembered, things that get measured get done. This is something that can and should be done on a regular basis with our employees, colleagues, and teams as well.

Sometimes we need to discipline those on our team because we must draw the line on what is acceptable behavior or to reinforce performance expectations. It is possible to do this in a way that is respectful and developmental as Bud Harrelson did with Gregg Jeffries in 1990 when he fined him for not showing respect to his coaches or manager (see Chapter 3), or we may need to bench an All-Star because he is not showing his teammates (and coaches) that he always puts forth 100% effort, whether or not the game is on the line. In baseball as well as in business we need to always remind ourselves and our people that there is always another move to be made, and we must keep pushing. We need to be consistent with the expectations that have been established, ensure the expectations become part of daily operations, and when an employee shows improvement, we need to acknowledge the specific change in order to reinforce the desirable behavior.

You got to have some sort of discipline or set of rules to obey that are common to everybody, that way there's no preferential treatment.

Jose Bautista, outfielder, Toronto Blue Jays

Challenges are Expected

If leadership were easy, everyone could do it. Leading people is challenging because it is a constant balance between the needs of your people and the needs of the business. You may face challenges related to unmotivated or unengaged team members or conflicts among members or other departments. Some team members will consistently exceed expectations while others never seem to live up to their potential. People have their quirks and effectively managing all the aspects of the various personalities adds to a leader's daily challenge, but also leads to some of the greatest rewards when positive change is seen.

I never want anybody to do my dirty work for me because [the players will] lose respect for me and they'll gain respect for the person who is doing the dirty work. In that respect, that's my job as a manager, to do that kind of dirty work. There will be times when coaches get upset in the dugout and say something or whatever, but when you're addressing the group or you're addressing an individual about something, I think that needs to come from me.

Bob Melvin, manager, Oakland Athletics

Joe Maddon had quite a situation when he arrived in Tampa Bay in 2005. The Devil Rays, as they were known until 2007, had been unsuccessful and many acknowledged that it was challenging to recognize the club as being a professional baseball team in their early years. After coaching and managing with the Los Angeles Angels and experiencing success for many years, coming to a team like the Devil Rays was a huge adjustment for Maddon, but he was up for the challenge and looked forward to being a change agent in Tampa. Joe shared that, "They had no idea. They really thought that just showing up, putting on a uniform, flying on chartered airplanes, and making minimum salary was a big league experience. There was so much to overcome there." He set out to change the culture and had to make some difficult decisions to eliminate team members who did not fit in with the new way of thinking. Maddon's success in changing the culture, and in turn the deliverables of the Tampa Bay (Devil) Rays, was rewarded with winning seasons and with personal accomplishments such as winning the American League Manager of the Year two times. Similar situations occur in the corporate world when a new leader arrives and it is up to them to assess their players, assess who is a 'fit', and determine who is not. Those who are not on board and not willing to invest the time and energy into making a change can sometimes be engaged with the many *Bases of Leadership* we've discussed, but sometimes may no longer be the right fit for the organization once the "Devil" comes out.

I don't know if it's my BS degree in mathematics, but I love solving problems. The harder the problem, the more I like it. I'm not a procrastinator, so when a problem comes up, I like it. You can call it tunnel vision, you can call it anything you want, but I like to focus every aspect that I can possibly think of and resolve that problem.

Davey Johnson, manager, Washington Nationals

Sometimes a leader has a great situation, a banner year, perhaps breaking sales records, achieving every goal, and turning an amazing profit. It seems that nothing can go wrong and the team is operating at the highest possible performance level. This is also a time to be somewhat cautious because it is possible that the situation, with little or no warning, may take a turn for the worse. The Milwaukee Brewers had an outstanding season in 2011, winning 96 games and earning a place in the playoffs by winning the National League Central title, but just a year later, with virtually the same team; they struggled to get 83 wins and came in third for their division. As Ron Roenicke shared with us, challenges, and trying to make corrections takes time, "How do you correct, or how do you turn around a season that's going the wrong way? We're fighting with that right now so there's a lot more thinking going on. This year, no doubt, I've had to do a lot more planning and thinking than I had to do last year. Last year I had to do a lot, but this year, because I'm trying to correct things, and I think, when things are going well you really, you're just trying to steer them in the right way. But when things are going bad, you can't just like steer them in the right way, you have to figure out how to get them back the right way. And there are more conversations with guys, more trying to build them up, there's a whole bunch of things that you have to do to try and figure out in the bad times, try to figure out how you get that player back and performing. And it's all about them performing. God has blessed us all with certain abilities; our job is to get those abilities out of the player. A lot of times it's the mental part of it, a lot of times it's the physical part of it. But to get that guy to the level of whatever his skill set is, that's the challenging part. Just like with this team right now. We're better than what we're playing. So myself and the coaches are trying to figure out, how do we go about, how do we get these guys back to where they're back at that level they should be. There are some players that are really struggling, and they haven't struggled this much before." Facing challenges and becoming an agent of positive change is one of the more difficult components of leadership, but when you can correct the course and get the ship headed in the right direction, it is very satisfying.

Managing the Game

If we revisit the basic tenets of management, we find plan, organize, direct, and control. These are the nuts and bolts, so to speak, of getting the job done. While we like to think more in terms of innovation, strategy, and influence when thinking of leadership, the basics also need to be addressed. Most people are more comfortable around preparation and order than they are in an environment of uncertainty and chaos. It is the responsibility of the leadership team to ensure people feel there is a rhyme and reason to what happens in the workplace. The same was found to be true with Major League Baseball. Bob Melvin shared his opinion on this, "The players also need to know that things are done in an orderly fashion, you're prepared, you're on time, and players play accordingly based on how prepared they feel like their team is on any particular day when you go out there." Isn't that how we all feel? Ned Yost, as Manager of the Kansas City Royals, shares the same philosophy, "We're extremely organized here. When our players walk in, it doesn't matter what time they walk in, they know exactly what they're doing from the second they walk in until the second they walk out. I think that's very important. I think confusion is something that we want to totally eliminate. So I want the players to know exactly what they're gonna do from the minute they walk in to the minute they walk out because in order to become a champion, you have to be focused. And if you don't know what you're doing, your focus starts to waver."

Many executives seek these qualities when hiring a leader for their organization. Gerry Hunsicker, who was the Vice President of the Tampa Bay Rays at the time of our interview, mentioned several important qualities that he seeks when identifying field managers for the organizations he has been involved with. The top attributes Hunsicker identified were professionalism, organization, and intelligence. He also noted that it was important for leaders to be versatile, have great people skills, and ultimately, be a good partner with the organization (ie, the executives off the field).

I think a manager here has got to be organized and pay attention to detail.
Terry Ryan, General Manager, Minnesota Twins

Jim Duquette, former GM for the New York Mets and current co-host of "Power Alley" on Sirius XM's MLB Network, has had the opportunity to work with many managers and observe a lot of baseball over the years. With that observation comes some very interesting insights as to how managers affect the win-loss record. He said, "Joe [Maddon] has a chance to impact their day and their game every single day by the way he makes up the lineup and then how he uses his pitchers and relievers. Every single game he has a feel and a touch on winning that ball game." He also provided examples of how Bruce Bochy and Tony La Russa manage the game during the regular season, and then a bit differently in the post-season. Situational leadership, understanding that situations necessitate different strategy and different styles of leadership is important to get the most from your team.

If you're not prepared and you're just winging it, they're gonna see right through you. It doesn't matter if you have a name or you don't have a name, they're not gonna believe in you.

Manny Acta, manager, Cleveland Indians

Achieve and Maintain Expertise

In this chapter we examined the importance of *knowing your game*. First, we identified the need to acquire the fundamental "hard skills" necessary to lead effectively. Second, the importance of gaining the necessary expertise within your organization and industry so you can have the deeper knowledge needed for decision-making was discussed. Third, we came to understand that leadership is about performance, and that typically requires discipline and consistency to establish appropriate expectations. The notion that leadership is not without challenges and that we must embrace these challenges in order to become a true agent of change was explored. Finally, we looked at the idea that becoming a result-oriented leader is about organization and execution.

As you seek to become a more effective leader in this area, a good place to start is to examine your personal definition of hard and soft skills and then list and evaluate your skills in each category. Ask yourself where you lean the most and if or how you integrate the two skill sets into your leadership. If there are gaps, identify what you might want to do to fill the gaps and the type of experience or coaching you may need to achieve your goals. For example, would it be helpful to volunteer for a developmental assignment? Also, think about anyone that might be in your network who could coach or mentor you in specific areas. Determine something about your industry that you desire to learn about and determine the best methods for studying your industry and becoming a subject matter expert. The time you spend investing in yourself will greatly reward you for years to come.

A trip to the mound...

- What are the fundamental skills that are required in my position and what are the gaps needing to be filled?

- How deep is my expertise in my field?

- Am I measuring and tracking the most important performance indicators for my department?

- Do I effectively address conflict so we can move forward?

- What areas of strategy execution can I develop further and who might partner with me to do this?

Chapter 9
Foster Teamwork

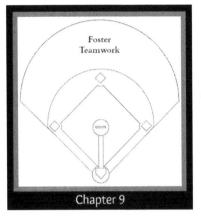

Foster
Teamwork

Chapter 9

To me the biggest joy for a manager is seeing a player play up to his potential. You win with twenty-five; you don't win with fifteen; so all twenty-five have to play to their capabilities. If they do, and you've got the talent, you win.

Davey Johnson, manager, Washington Nationals

To this point we've discussed those individual behaviors which help a team become successful. We talked about the passion of the leader, the need to develop strong relationships, the benefit of mutual respect, and the importance of recognizing and appreciating your people as individuals. In this chapter we will discuss that no matter how successful a leader is with all the above, if he or she can't empower the team to work together as a unit, the individual successes won't always lead to the actual goal, team or organizational success. As the great Babe Ruth said, 'The way a team plays as a whole determines its success. You may have the greatest bunch of individual stars in the world, but if they don't play together, the club won't be worth a dime'[18]. In the following pages we'll delve into how leaders can encourage their team to do just that, to play together and achieve collective greatness.

It's a Team Effort!

In the workplace the term 'team' is used quite often as many of us belong to teams based around projects, reporting structure, etc. A baseball team, though encompassing some different 'parts', has many similarities as well. To be most successful a team should be comprised of pieces which are focused on a common goal but hold different areas of expertise. In baseball we have players who play different positions, and in the workplace we have (or should have) people who come from different backgrounds and have different strengths, thus playing different positions on the team. Effective teams in baseball, we have seen and written about here, are the ones which keep it 'light' in the clubhouse, but are serious when they need to be. Teams which have fun with each other and truly 'know' their team mates are the ones which when are on the field can be most comfortable as they know the strengths and limitations of their counterparts across the diamond. If you are making a tough play on third base and know your first baseman has great range you will be more apt to make a quick throw knowing that your team mate has the ability to make a scoop if needed and make the out. If, however, you know your first baseman has a pulled hamstring and just got off the disabled list, perhaps you should 'eat it', and not attempt a play that could lead to the ball ending up in the outfield and the runner taking second. OK, that's enough baseball talk for now, what does this mean in business? Well, quite simply, if you are working on a project you deem important but you know that your counterpart is overloaded, it is probably best to wait for the appropriate time to pitch your idea so that it gets the attention it needs. As we've discussed throughout *Lead Me Out to the Ballgame*, to be successful you need to know your people and know the situation that you are in.

In baseball we often think of the team as encompassing a pitcher, a catcher, infielders, and outfielders, but in actuality there are many more pieces to the puzzle which need to be considered. Let's first consider the leader, the manager. This is a formal role, but in order for the team to follow the leader unequivocally a relationship needs to be fostered. A manager who takes pride in his team's accomplishments, both wins and efforts, and shares this pride publicly, will be more embraced by his players and coaches more so than one who simply looks for the win.

There are many behind the scenes roles which are played on teams, both in baseball and in other organizations. In addition to the formal roles or positions a team needs people who will fill certain functions. Think about teams you've been on:

- Are there 'roles' people play?

- Do you have cheerleaders for ideas?

- Do you have someone who asks a lot of questions thus clarifying concepts?

- Is there someone who seems to question everything and offer counter opinions and ideas?

- What about a jokester, someone who keeps the mood light, or a facilitator, someone who keeps the team on track?

These are just some of the roles which are useful on a team which assist in bringing forth ideas and working with them to come up with a solution or next steps to be taken.

I'm proud of my team and my players every day, my joy and my fun comes from watching them have success, my whole day is built around them. What can we do to make them better, what can we do to make them champions, and what can we do to help them be successful? Not only in the game of baseball, but in life.

Ned Yost, manager, Kansas City Royals

For a team to be most successful the leadership needs to be embodied by all its members. Let's remember that position is not what creates leaders, actions are. Each member of the team needs to act as a leader by showing care and concern not only for themselves, but for the overall goals of the team and for the contributions that each member will make towards achieving it. One of the ways that a baseball manager can 'share' his leadership is to utilize his coaching staff as well as his players to encourage the team message and excite each other towards their goals. The impact that the players have on each other shouldn't be understated. Just as the manager and coaches play a role in the reinforcement of a positive message, the players do this as well. Howie Kendrick, infielder for the Los Angeles Angels of Anaheim, had this to say about the impact of his teammates on failure, success, and the day to day grind, "when failure comes knocking, if you just throw in the towel, you're never going to get anywhere. So, I think the biggest thing about being able to persevere through the failure is that you just got to keep working and know that hey, there's going to be a light at the end of the tunnel. And just try to just keep rolling with everything. And I think the biggest thing is you have your teammates around to keep your morale up. Everybody here has been through rough spells, and you just got to keep pushing. I think that's one thing about this game, the good thing about it is you play every day and then the bad thing about it too is that you play every day"

As with any team, baseball or not, leaders need to be careful to delegate the right tasks to their people, and keep the right tasks for themselves. Ron Washington shared with us that as a manager, if he sees something he isn't happy with, he first turns to his coaches, and if the situation still isn't handled, he then deals with it himself. The coaches serve as a vital part of a team just as the middle managers serve a vital role in an organization, it's their job to transfer the message of the manager to the masses and it is their job to *live* the vision of the organization.

This philosophy isn't very different from a manager in the workplace allowing his staff to tackle an issue initially before he or she steps in to help remedy it. There are many reasons to deal with an issue like this, and one of them concerns team dynamics. It is important, as we have discussed, to empower all those people on your team and delegating responsibility is one way to do this. Bob Melvin, goes a little deeper in this regard telling us that for many things he turns to his coaching staff. He went further on to say that he never wants anyone to do the 'dirty work' for him, and with major issues he will tackle those himself, for as he said, 'that's his job as the manager'.

I'm trying to create an atmosphere but these guys are who really carry the message. Our pitching coach is doing his work with his guys, the hitting coach is doing his thing. We got guys working with infielders, outfielders, base running, so they're all doing individual jobs. You gotta have good players and you gotta have a great staff, and from there, it's a lot easier for you.

Don Mattingly, manager, Los Angeles Dodgers.

As much as managers lean on their coaches and players to serve as mentors, it is also important, as it is outside of baseball as well, that the *right* behaviors and attitudes are followed by younger players. Many of us can remember unsportsmanlike behaviors that we have seen both on and off the diamond; and it is important, as Brad Mills, Houston Astros manager, shared with us, to make sure that the younger players are looking up to and modeling their behavior after positive role models in the clubhouse. To do this inside or outside of baseball, it is important for managers, as well as people at all the ranks, to validate those people who are demonstrating the behaviors which are desired by the organization. Those people who go out of their way for their teammates and the organization's mission should be publicly applauded for this so that others see the appreciation that acting in this manner will garner. Some players are seen as leaders not necessarily for their actions off the field but for their accomplishments on the field. This type of leadership can be dangerous as it relates not to the behaviors which the organization wants mimicked, but to the outcomes. When a player (or an employee) has a strong presence sometimes it is important for the manager to reinforce the message that they must model the appropriate behaviors since they are being followed (whether they want to be or not). Bud Harrelson, former manager of the New York Mets, recounted for us a situation when he had to approach one of his All Stars about modeling the right behavior and being a more positive leader on the team. Harrelson told us, "I brought Strawberry in and I said 'You're a leader.' And he goes 'yeah, yeah.' And I said 'No, yeah, yeah.' I said, 'When you come and you don't work, you don't take BP[8], you don't take fly balls, you're not ready to play, guys know it, and you bring the team down. But when you come and you're enthusiastic and you're doing your job you lift this team because they're depending upon you to have a good day. You come and do your work you go 0 for 4, it's okay. You come and don't do your work and you're 0 for 4, it's bad. You {need to} lead by example.' I was educating him."

The ability to have champions and leaders in different areas of an organization is a great benefit in teams in general as a message can be conveyed differently (and thus received differently) from a peer than from a supervisor. Having people as champions throughout the organization serves a great purpose for the manager as well, as these champions can articulate the pulse of what is going on with the team to the manager and help the manager to address issues when needed. The champions serve as an amplifier to others of the team or organization's goals and as support and mentorship for younger

---

[8] Batting Practice

or newer members. Gio Gonzalez, Washington Nationals pitcher, who at the time of our interview was in his 3rd year of major league service, reiterated the thoughts of many of the 'younger' players about leadership in the clubhouse. It's not just the manager who players turn to for advice and guidance, Gonzalez shared, it's also the 'veteran guys or the coaches. The guys who've had years of experience that know what they're saying and know what they're doing. Our job is to go out there and listen and try to take what they've experienced, pass it down, and try to do the same thing.' Veterans throughout the game echoed this sentiment, acknowledging, as Carl Pavano of the Twins did that it is the manager's job to manage personalities, but 'as you become a veteran on the team, as a teammate, that's part of your job too.'

Managers need to know their strengths and just as importantly they need to know the strengths of those around them. Ron Gardenhire, manager of the Minnesota Twins, was forthright in telling us that there are certain areas of the game that he doesn't know everything about, and when it comes to those areas he turns to others for advice and direction. CEOs and corporate executives are lucky when they have boards of directors filled with experts in their fields, and Ron Gardenhire is lucky to have his predecessor, former manager Tom Kelly[9] as someone to lean on and garner advice from. Managers throughout the league expressed to us that there is a reason that they have coaches on their staff, and it is up to the coaches to field questions and help their players excel in their areas of expertise. Bud Harrelson, former manager of the New York Mets shared with us that when he took over as manager of the Mets (when longtime fan favorite and now retired manager of the Nationals, Davey Johnson, was fired) one of the

---

[9] Tom Kelly managed the Minnesota Twins from 1986-2001 leading them to World Series victories in 1987 and 1991. Kelly won the Manager of the Year award in the American League in 1991.

first things he did was tell his veteran pitching coach Mel Stottlemyre, 'We have 25 guys, I'm giving you 10, I got the other 15.' He handed off the pitchers to the expert and focused on helping his position players with what he knew best, batting practice, infield drills, and the like.

It would be silly for me to try to take over and run the show in pitching or anything like that, I have pitching coaches. The biggest thing you do as a manager is trust.

Ron Gardenhire , manager, Minnesota Twins

Focusing on the Goals

To build and foster a successful team a manager needs to help each individual realize, commit to, and stay focused on their common goals. As the head coach of the 1980 USA Hockey 'Miracle' team, Herb Brooks said, 'When you pull on that jersey, you represent yourself and your teammates, and the name on the front is a hell of a lot more important than the name on the back.' Once you are a part of a team, once you are a part of any organization, you need to realize that your efforts need to go into the success of the whole ... not the success of the individual. The simple truth is that a manager's job is to empower his or her team by setting goals and direction and by helping team members to understand the best way for them to reach their goals. In baseball, one would think this would be easy, with the goal each day being to win games. As we have uncovered, there is much more that goes into a successful season than simply winning games. One of the keys in the creation of an effective team is for each member of the team to realize the value that they contribute to it. Whether you are the starting pitcher or the backup to the backup third baseman, you play an important part in the team dynamic, both on and off the field.

As Manny Acta, Cleveland Indians manager, told us that no player should get preferential treatment, the letters on the front of the jersey are what are most important, not the ones on the back. It's important to always remember that games aren't only won on the field, a baseball team is comprised of 25 players; and the ones who are in the dugout and bullpen are in the clubhouse with the starting nine before and after each game...they are a part of the team and need to remember that their attitudes and their input does not go unnoticed.

In the world outside of baseball sometimes individual goals can be blurred as employees may not understand how their particular actions impact the overall success of their organizations. It is vital for managers throughout the ranks to spend time reinforcing to their people at all levels how whatever job they are doing contributes significantly to the overall goals of the organization. Think about your own organization, do you know how what you do *directly* relates to the strategic goal of the organization (taking that further, do you know *what* the strategic goal of your organization is?). Well, you should. If you are a teacher your goal is to turn the material you are given (your students) into better contributors for society. If you are a doctor you are tasked to help your patients and thus help your practice bring new patients in for treatment (via word of mouth); if you are a maintenance worker your job is to help keep the facilities clean and running smoothly so that the people who utilize them will have a pleasant experience, thus helping them to do their jobs and provide their services to customers. No matter what you do you must know why it is important, without this you will not feel a part of the team and not contribute your all for the team. Without the 25th man on the roster the starting third baseman may not feel comfortable taking a hard slide into second for fear that if he got hurt the team wouldn't have a backup at his position...each player plays an important role for the success of the team and the manager must make this absolutely clear.

The big thing is getting the guys to all come together with one goal in mind.

Mike Aviles, infielder, Boston Red Sox

Let's have some Fun

One of the ways to help a team become more cohesive and to reinforce its commitment to the overall goals is through bonding or team building exercises. These activities can range from taking a team to play paintball to a workshop where teams can, as a group, learn new concepts or techniques. One way that Joe Maddon, two-time Manager of the Year, likes his team to bond is by having fun and laughing at one another at the same time. Maddon instills a sense of fun in his clubhouse, and as SiriusXM host Mike Ferrin told us, he lets his boys be boys. Pablo Sandoval, infielder, San Francisco Giants, certainly likes to have fun in the clubhouse. During our day with the Giants, we observed Sandoval 'encouraging' rookies to get in the laundry cart because 'that was what everyone did.' He chased them around the clubhouse for at least 15 minutes, laughing, and having a great time. He didn't manage to get anyone into the cart, but the message was received loud and clear, there's a time to be serious, but there's always time for fun!

It's baseball, you have to have fun! I'm the kind of guy who comes to a field, has fun the most that I can. Just give it to my friends, my teammates, all the fun stuff we can do to relax a little bit to play the game.
Pablo Sandoval, infielder, San Francisco Giants

The themed road trips that Maddon arranges for his team have become a well-known example of Maddon's unique approach to leadership. Numerous times throughout the baseball season Maddon encourages the Rays to dress up when they travel to various cities to take on their rivals. One player, Brandon Guyer, expressed what seems to be the sentiment of Maddon's players, "I think they're really cool. That's the first time I've ever had something like that. It builds team camaraderie; it just shows how laid back and fun it is here." Maddon shared with us that some of his favorite themed trips included the team wearing letterman sweaters and dressing in pajamas on a flight to the West Coast (he pointed out that many ordered their 'onesies' ahead of time!). More recently Maddon orchestrated a 'Nerd Trip' and the team really enjoyed dressing in bow ties and suspenders! When we asked Joe if he participated in the themed trips (i.e., did he dress up with the team), his response came quickly, 'absolutely! I embrace it!'

It's not just the managers who see the value in having fun. As Tampa Bay Rays outfielder shared about his manager, Joe Maddon, "He sets the atmosphere in the clubhouse and by keeping it loose and relaxed it really plays to guys' strengths. In baseball you have to relax. It's a game, and you have to relax. It's such a long season you have to have fun because you're here day in and day out. So if you're not laughing and joking, you're gonna get stressed, you're gonna get tense. And you fail so much in this game that it becomes a stressful scenario. So Joe's great about just understanding the whole mental aspect of baseball and what you go through as a player. I think that really benefits him and benefits us." Having fun as a team can have a great effect on the players. Adam LaRoche, infielder for the Washington Nationals, recounted for us a story of how a minor league manager of his, current Atlanta Braves third base coach Brian Snitker, tried to get him to 'wake up' by putting Red Bulls in his locker.

Certainly, as has been expressed to us throughout our interviews, the daily grind can be stressful for players, managers, coaches, and even fans. But let's now turn our focus to the daily grind of working in a Fortune 100 company, a Fortune 500 company, a nonprofit, or a family owned three person 'shop'; it doesn't matter what uniform you wear, no matter what you do to support yourself, you will sometimes become tired, stressed, and overwhelmed. What can those of us outside of baseball learn from the clubhouse to develop our *Major League Leadership*? We can learn that it is important to relax, have fun, and enjoy our colleagues, and this in turn will help us to get through the grind and thus perform better as a team and also individually. One of the companies which does this very well is Google where their offices has a 'clubhouse' feel with a slide, bowling alley, and more to help employees unwind and bond...perhaps a baseball diamond should be considered with their next round of renovations!

Why dress up as nerds or prank players? Why put Red Bulls in your player's locker? What's the purpose of participating in teambuilding events with your players (as Don Mattingly shared with us)? There are many reasons for this, as Joe Maddon explained, some being encouraging team unity, risk taking, and bonding. As Maddon noted, when you walk into a hotel in New York City dressed as a cowboy, it solidifies unity with your team. He wants his players to take risks together off the field so that they will do so on the field as well. He explained, "A big part is risk taking. I even had one player tell me at one time he loved it because of that purpose. He didn't say it was risk taking, but he said "I gotta dress in a way that I never do and I feel uncomfortable about it, but once I do it I kinda like it." And boom, that was perfect, that was a perfect response to me. So now when he goes out and pitches in the 8th inning and the bases are loaded, there might be a little more comfort derived in that moment because he's taking a risk doing something."

Another example of how managers and players can have fun with each other was told to us by veteran pitcher Carl Pavano and an experience he had with manager Jack McKeon in 2003. When McKeon took over as manager of the Florida Marlins, he felt that his players were leaving the dugout during the game a bit too often between innings. He told them, according to Pavano, that they should remain in the dugout unless it was absolutely necessary to leave. McKeon's point was well taken, the players should remain in the dugout, support their teammates, and watch the game so that they could develop and get better. That said, some of the younger guys wanted to have some fun with their new manager, so one of them made 'pee-pee and poopie' passes and hung the passes behind McKeon in the dugout. When the players now wanted to leave the dugout they would first take a pass. McKeon laughed, but his point was well taken, and the team followed the mantra of their manager, watch the game, learn the game, and go to the bathroom after the game! As a side note, McKeon managed those 2003 Marlins to second place in their division in his first year with the team.

When managers joke around with their team it encourages their team to have fun as well. The Washington Nationals are a team that has demonstrated this passionately over the short time that veteran manager Davey Johnson has been at the helm. Davey encourages individuality and encourages his players to do what they need to do to be successful without succumbing to the pressures brought upon them from off the field. Davey does not like to make work for the sake of making work. He wants his players on the field and at the gym so that they can be best prepared, not so the Press can say, 'look how well Davey preps his team'. Johnson's spring training workouts with his players are often shorter than the ones his counterparts facilitate, but they are structured in a way that the players work hard, work fast, and work smart … all things that the players appreciate.

Having a manager like Davey Johnson who doesn't succumb to pressure and encourages individuality has led to some high jinks in Nationals Park and other parks around the league. One of the traditions in the short history of the Washington Nationals has been the 'Racing

Presidents' during National's home games. The Presidents, Roosevelt, Lincoln, Washington, and Jefferson all race during the 4th inning of each home game, and up until 2012, Teddy Roosevelt had yet to win a race. The fact that Teddy had never won a race, and the Washington Nationals had never had a winning season, is a relationship that didn't go unnoticed by the Nationals players. Washington Post columnist Tom Boswell shared with us a story that in 2011 the Nationals players decided to do something about this injustice. Boswell recounted, "the players decided, 'You know, we've been a losing team ever since we came to Washington and we're sick of Teddy losing. We want Teddy to win, just like we want to win.' One night the entire bullpen jumps out of the bullpen as the racing president's come around the warning track and tackle everybody but Teddy. The bullpen ambush all the presidents, knock them all down, and pin them to the ground. The Teddy mascot doesn't know what to do. He's not supposed to win. And so he falls down and pretends to be down, and Davey loves that! Players didn't feel like they had to run it by him, but Davey thought that was great. He wants them to goof around."

The Nationals came close to a winning season in 2011, finishing with a record of 80 wins and 81 losses, but in 2012 still under the leadership of Davey Johnson, they won the division for the first time in their history, and Teddy won a few races as well! The lightheartedness that LaRoche, Pavano, and others talked about serves a great purpose to them and to the team as a whole. Toronto Blue Jays All Star, Jose Bautista, summed it up nicely for us, 'you always [have to] keep the guys happy and loose, that way you don't have players that are going on to the field afraid of making a mistake.'

Baseball is Fun! As a kid, playing little league is fun. A high school student playing baseball for his school is fun. A college player, representing their alma mater is fun. Thus, playing professional baseball should be even more fun! The pressure of winning, however, having to deal with the press, having to take long trips and sleep in hotels for 230 days out of the year, and having to manage yourself through tough situations, well, sometimes the fun can be forgotten. That, according to many we spoke with, is where the manager, the leader, comes in. The manager doesn't need to always make grand gestures to instill a sense of camaraderie in his team, sometimes something as simple as organizing a team dinner (with the manager 'footing the bill' as Darren Oliver, pitcher for the Toronto Blue Jays told us) can be great for team building. The key isn't necessarily what the manager does, it's that the manager does something to bring his people together and allow them to be themselves. It's noteworthy that on a baseball team, just as in a business setting, people are all busy doing 'their' jobs each day and working with the people who they most often deal with. In industry this can mean the marketing department spending most of their time working together but not spending much time with their counterparts in operations or finance; and in baseball this can mean the infielders working with each other but not interacting with the pitchers very often. As the organization is working towards a common goal whether the employee is housed in the outfield or the HR department, it is important that the team spend time together understanding the importance of the job that everyone within the organization does. As Mike Aviles of the Red Sox told us, "sometimes in baseball I think you get separated, pitchers and catchers and hitters and position players." He explained that after doing drills and exercises in their respective groups it's important and appreciated when the manager brings the team together as a whole as well.

Once you start detracting the kid from what you're doing here, once you think it's all business and you're not, you can't have fun and be successful.

Joe Maddon, manager, Tampa Bay Rays

Donnie Baseball, Dodger's manager Don Mattingly, remembers the long trips and the pressure of playing each and every day from when he was an All Star on the New York Yankees. He also remembers the fun he had when he played little league and makes sure to remind his players of that feeling as well. Mattingly knows the responsibilities his players feel, he understands the amount of money on the line, the competition they feel, and the business side of the game. With that, however, he reminds his team that each day they should have some fun in the mornings, keep the trips light, and keep the fun going when they get to the ballpark (but at the same time get down to business).

Make it Fun

The message to have fun in what you do is essential in the long term success of an organization as well as for the long term success of an individual. In baseball, as we have been discussing, as bad a day as you are having, you are still doing something you've loved for most of your life. At work, this isn't always the case which is why we need to find ways to make it fun. One of the ways managers both inside and outside of baseball can do this is by encouraging competition amongst team members. The issue around this is that in order for competition to be a positive team building and motivational tool it must be a part of a positive organizational culture (which relates to our tenth *Base of Leadership* and will be discussed in Chapter 10). Competition amongst employees can be positive if it is used for self-improvement and can also lead to enhanced team dynamics if teams are created to compete against each other. An example of this can be in sales, operations processing, marketing plans, etc. A bit of competition between individuals, as well as teams, can be used to motivate and inspire employees to learn how to improve themselves so that they can achieve success amongst their peers. In the baseball clubhouse this is done with contests relating to speed, accuracy, and even strength. Players, as well as coaches, encourage their team mates while pushing themselves as they know that by improving themselves (and 'winning' a competition here and there) they will be benefitting their team as well.

Having a strong team dynamic, as opposed to a strong culture of individual performers, is important for the long term success of any organization, baseball or otherwise. As we've discussed in this chapter as well as others, it begins with the top, the leaders setting the tone, and is fostered throughout the ranks by the managers, coaches, and players 'living' the ideals. The ways we can foster this are by finding ways to encourage fun in the work we do, encouraging all to participate in activities, and empowering each member of the team to be a leader in all they do. This *Base of Leadership* interacts with each of the others as if the others are incorporated into the workplace then the team dynamic will be strong.

A trip to the mound...

- Am I spending enough time with my 'utility players' so that they know their value on the team?

- Are my advocates helping me to spread my ideas to the rest of the team?

- Do team members trust and know they can count on their colleagues?

- Are all members of the team aware of our overall goal and how their individual contributions factor into that goal?

- What team building activity can I organize that will engage the specific personalities I have on my team?

Chapter 10
Create a Winning Culture

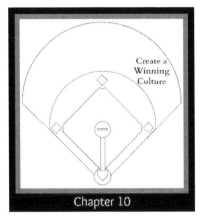

Chapter 10

What I'm most proud of is the culture change, the belief in how it should be done, and then going out there and doing everything they can to make it work and make it happen.

Ron Washington, manager, Texas Rangers

An organization's culture includes the values, norms, and social relationships within it. Members of the organization, the leadership vision, and environmental factors influence the culture, which then influences modes of operating, strategy, and goals. In fact, Peter Drucker was known for stating that "culture eats strategy for breakfast." This is a great indicator of the importance that culture plays in an organization's ultimate success. Zappos is known for exceptional customer service and their core values reflect this: Deliver WOW through service, Embrace and Drive Change, Build a Positive Team and Family Spirit, Be Passionate and Determined, and Be Humble – to highlight a few[19]. Southwest Airlines has a vision "To become the World's Most Loved, Most Flown, and Most Profitable Airline" and they drive behaviors to support this through their values of: Warrior Spirit, Servant's Heart, Fun-LUVing Attitude, and Work the Southwest Way[20].

In baseball, that culture often embodies the spirit of winning – the desire to be a part of something greater than your own performance and accolades. Craig Breslow, as a pitcher for the Diamondbacks, articulated it in this manner, "there's also just playing to try to start to build this feeling of winning that guys that younger guys and guys that were going to come up in September could start to buy into. Come spring training, you have this culture of winning that was developed the year before. So I think it's important to understand that while winning is the greatest motivator in my mind, at the highest level, I guess winning doesn't necessarily mean the same thing to everyone." This culture of winning can be especially challenging in a sport where winning 50% of the time is a good season or getting a hit 3/10 times at bat places you in a category of a great hitter. This equates to more days with losses than days with wins. Players need to believe they are in the right place and enjoy their club. As Brad Mills stated, "I think you always try to create an atmosphere within that clubhouse, on a daily basis, that is one that the guys want to be around, and that they want to be a part of."

In this chapter we will examine what it takes to develop a winning culture. First, we will define culture by looking at what we value, believe, and do. Next, we will examine how our vision for the future provides us with an ultimate destination to reach as well as how the strategy that we develop creates a roadmap to our destination. We will also look at how to measure our success and ultimately, how to develop a winning culture for your organization.

Defining and Creating Culture

Culture is complex for it is made of a pattern of dynamic relationships and depends on the beliefs and attitudes of the organization's members. The collective and individual behavior of the members creates the cultural norms that include habits, values, and customs. Such behaviors could include simple things we do together as a team such as going out to lunch together for someone's birthday or doing a special chant after a home run. The behaviors also include specific ways that we work with customers such as timely and skillful follow up to concerns and special discounts on milestone anniversaries. The behaviors that people observe become what the organization is known for and we strive to have that align with our stated core values, vision, and mission.

Being rooted in values and belief systems makes changing a culture a challenging but not insurmountable task. This is where leaders have to be clear and strong and purposeful because it is not easy to change a culture or build a culture that will be the foundation for the organization's success. Internal and external critics will try to pull the change off course and the Skipper must be mindful of this and have a strategy to remain steadfast. Joe Maddon, discussed how challenging this is as a manager, but that not living up to this challenge can lead to failure, "So when you're building a culture like we have, you're going to have to be prepared to absorb a lot of criticism if you truly stick with what you believe is the right way to do things. Criticism normally comes from outside the building or the organization, talk radio or something somebody might write in a newspaper. And I believe the organizations that really gauge or create their policies based on that are really setting themselves up for the fall. If you don't adhere to the group or the leadership within the group and run these ideas off each other and eventually come to your core conclusions, you're going to fail."

So when you're building a culture like we have, you're going to have to be prepared to absorb a lot of criticism. Joe Maddon, manager, Tampa Bay Rays

Passion is the heart that pumps life into our leadership each day and the passion a leader has will be influential in shaping the culture of the organization. Similarly, our values establish the baseline of what we believe and how we behave; together, this enables us to truly lead by example by living our values. Culture is truly the marriage and living example of our passion and values. We must care. We must believe. We must have alignment with what we hold to be true and good. This synergy will drive our behaviors and create expectations that become the cultural norms within our organization. This is not simple because there will be people both within and outside our organization who do not possess the same passion or hold the same values. Our challenge as leaders is to stay the course and ensure that the culture is shaped in the image we envision.

Changing an existing culture takes time and diligence. Creating a winning culture requires that we actually focus on winning. That doesn't mean that everything we do and say is centered on competition but rather success and how we define it. We must create an environment that is conducive to accomplishing what we define as success. Doing this takes effort and commitment. Ron Washington shared his thoughts on changing the culture in Texas, "Bring that attitude, bring that effort, and bring that commitment, every day, and we'll be here more than we'll be there. So that's what I'm most proud of, changing the culture around here. I really am, not so much that we won in 2010 and we won last year, because we didn't finish it off. But what I'm most proud of is the culture change, the belief in how it should be done. And then going out there and doing everything they can to make it work and make it happen."

To me the ultimate motivation should be winning.

Craig Breslow, pitcher, Arizona Diamondbacks

Winning may be defined differently depending on goals and expectations. A team that spends top payroll dollars to put together an all-star team may not be satisfied with 100 wins – they only want a pennant. However, a team with limited payroll may find reason to celebrate exceeding expectations; although, they will always enjoy celebrating a pennant! It does seem that when we are able to accomplish more than was expected, especially with limited resources, it can make the victory even sweeter. Manny Acta shared with us what it was like his first year as a Major League Manager in such a situation: "I was especially proud as it was my first year in Washington DC where the team was projected to win between 35-40 games and we ended up winning 73 games and not finishing dead last as everybody was picking us to. And especially because the talent, it wasn't there. It was just a couple of guys and then a bunch of guys that we brought to spring training; they meshed really well, finished up strong. We felt pretty proud at the end of the season and thought about Toby Keith's song there "How do you like me now?" When you say we're gonna win 40 games and we win 73 games and I was very proud, especially because that was my first year managing at the big league level."

Ensuring you have the desired culture requires that you also have an environment of trust and that requires character. This means we are honest and transparent in all of our interactions both internally and externally. Herb Kelleher of Southwest Airlines has used trust to create a culture of empowerment and this culture has helped them become not only profitable but also highly admired. Bud Black, manager of the San Diego Padres, told us that, "You have to create an environment where people want to work, people want to come to work, and people have the ability to be themselves. And again, the empowerment of your organization of the people is very important. For me, it's important for Padres baseball to have that, for any, whether you're the Braves, the Tigers, doesn't matter, an environment where winning is the goal, is to win a world championship and create a positive environment where that is what everybody's reaching for."

There must also be collaboration among team members because winning cultures share common goals. Team building occurs when people have the opportunity to work together and this strengthens alignment and the focus on goal achievement. Creating a winning culture also requires understanding where we want to go and how we will get there – the vision and the strategy – and remaining performance focused so we will achieve our desired results.

The Vision is Our Destination

A vision is a glimpse of the future. It is where we are going; our destination. A great vision will answer a wide variety of questions, such as:

- What are we known for?

- What does our organization look like?

- How big are we?

- What is our scope?

- Why is what we do important?

- What do our employees really think about us?

- Do we make a difference?

Keep in mind that the vision is not your strategy but it does help us to understand where the strategic plan is taking us. While the strategies may shift to align with or get in front of market and environmental changes, the vision will remain the same. John Farrell stressed that making the vision personal so that each person understands their role, and understands how the vision becomes a part of them is critical, "What do they want to be known for? What is their legacy? What do they want to leave behind? I want them to be able to tell a story, and that story is that they went out and they worked together. Collectively, they achieved a goal together, and they would be remembered for that, and not just the name on their back."

[it's important to] be able to communicate your vision and expectations to the group and where we're going collectively.
John Farrell, manager, Toronto Blue Jays

Leadership vision influences the organization's culture. Major League Baseball managers are often referred to as the "Skipper" and that provides a great analogy when discussing vision. As Skipper, the manager is at the helm and guiding the ship (team) toward their ultimate destination. What this destination is and finding ways to communicate the vision often and in relevant ways is very important to keeping it real. Brad Mills, addressed this from the team and individual perspective, "… have a vision in front of them, of what we're trying to accomplish, and put that in front of them on a daily basis. Put that vision and how we're trying to play with enthusiasm, play with energy, and play good, solid baseball. That's our goal, and keep that in front of them every day, and talk to each one of them about that."

The vision should be exciting and full of possibilities. A carefully crafted vision will draw upon the hopes and dreams of everyone involved with the organization. It is through knowing your people and having great relationships with them that allow exceptional leaders the ability to tap into these hopes and dreams and link them to the vision of the organization. This is accomplished through deep connections through people so that we can share a common vision and mutually achieve our dreams. Mike Scioscia, Los Angeles Angels of Anaheim manager, talked about what it was like playing for someone who could truly create a shared vision of wining. Scioscia said, "Tommy Lasorda, he was the only manager I would play for and he's really a master for setting that environment we're talking about. He did it in a little different way than I think I do it, but bottom line was there's an environment where you thought you were going to play and you were going to win. And I think that's critical to give a team or give a player that vision."

I firmly believe that players win games and it's my job to put them in a situation where they'll be successful, if I do that then I'm doing a good job.

Davey Johnson, manager, Washington Nationals

A vision of success, of winning, requires competing every day. The definition of what it means to compete, or even to win, may vary according to industry, but we can all relate to it and know it when we see it. In the business world, we can't just compete on Thursdays or in the spring, we must compete year-round. You must not only understand your vision but also that of your competitors and it is important that you grasp the intricacies of your industry and maintain a healthy respect for the business you are in because it helps you to focus on the long-term vision. Brad Mills, addressed this subject during our interview, "The desire to compete every day is the biggest thing. In my opening talk this year I talked about competing and respecting the game. One thing is, if you compete to beat the other club, you are respecting the game of baseball, and that's the best way to go about it. If you respect the person, your teammates and the game, you're gonna compete, and you're gonna play hard, and you're gonna have a lot of energy. If we can get guys to understand respecting the game, respecting each other, and respecting the team, the name that's on the front of the jersey, you're a lot better off."

A vision can only be achieved if people know what it is, understand it, and know how to get there. Being a great leader requires that we have a vision that is well communicated. It cannot just sit on a shelf or appear on the website. The vision must be well known and become part of the vernacular of the organization. A great vision is inspiring – but must be heard in order to evoke inspiration. John Farrell shared this about vision, "We have to create an identity within this group and the sooner we can grasp what those characteristics are, [the sooner] that identity will evolve. I think it's important for them to know what the vision is, from my standpoint." Right at the beginning, Farrell ensured he not only communicated the vision, but also how they would go about attaining it.

The "how" portion is more about the strategy – the organization's goals and objectives. Again, the vision is our destination but the strategy will provide us with the roadmap to get there. We cannot be successful without both the destination and the map.

The Strategy is Our Roadmap

Strategy, as well as the goals and objectives to achieve it, stems from the vision of the organization. The strategic plan tells us how we will reach our destination by outlining what we intend to achieve and how we will direct the organization and its resources toward accomplishing these goals. In basic terms, it describes how we are going to get things done. Strategic management is a core requirement for organizational success as it provides several advantages to the organization. It provides focus to the members and unifies the organization. It encourages management to be more proactive and promotes continuous evaluation and improvement of the business model while guiding decision making regarding budgets and other necessary resources.

In Major League Baseball, the strategy is communicated and reinforced from the first day of Spring Training. The tone of the season is established so everyone understands his part in the team. John Farrell stated, "That was at the outset of our spring training here, not only put a goal out there that's realistic, but I think at the same time, to give them what my thoughts are on how we're to go about our work. How we're to go about the way we play the game." Brad Mills has a similar philosophy and wanted to ensure that each member of the team understood this clearly so that each could say, "Hey, this is what we're trying to accomplish, and we can work together to accomplish that." These managers understand that they must create a culture of winning, have a clear vision for their future, establish a strategy and set goals for getting to their destination, and reinforce this each day by communicating it and living it.

Strategy formulation combines a future-oriented viewpoint with interest for the organization's internal and external environments. Organizations must take the utmost in care in assessing the internal environment as organizational resources and capabilities must complement the chosen strategy to enable success. Structure and organizational competencies must have "fit" since implementation is dependent upon the organization's ability to execute the plan. Sometimes this means that we may need to acquire new competencies or capabilities to achieve our goals. The organization must not only have the capability to execute but also the desire to implement change through a cultural shift. Appropriate leadership is a necessity to guide the organization's culture toward change and execution; thus, goal attainment.

Don Mattingly discussed the need to truly be a team in order to accomplish your goals and this includes ensuring that individual goals are consistent with team goals: "Well, you gotta be fair to people, it's good to have an understanding of what your goals are for the team. What you're trying to accomplish. Have an understanding that players are individually trying to accomplish things and then trying to blend that all and everybody together. Be able to take what they are trying to accomplish and also what we are trying to accomplish along with that. And have those two meld and have them come to an understanding that they can do both. And you having a great year helps us as a team. But there are times where the team has to be first, trying to win a game. That's what people come to see, is your team to win."

When developing your organization's strategy, there are many approaches to take. Each approach involves some sort of strategic analysis where you look at the vision, note where you are today, determine the gap, and then consider what needs to be accomplished to fill the gap. Various tools and techniques can assist leaders in this process. A very common practice is to use a SWOT Analysis where the internal strengths and weaknesses as well as the external opportunities and threats are examined. Another approach is critical issue analysis to determine root causes, categorize obstacles, classify strengths to leverage, and identify key people in the organization. Many organizations find that taking a team approach, consisting of various levels of organizational stakeholders, with the assistance of a designated facilitator, can expedite the strategic planning process while gaining institutional buy in. Regardless of the approach that is used, it is important that several important questions be answered: who are we, where is our market, how do we operate, what are our capabilities, and how will we measure success?

In Major League Baseball, the General Manager carries a lot of the strategic responsibility because he is the one controlling most of the player contract decisions and that affects the team's capabilities. At the manager level, decisions are more tactical and day-to-day. Jim Duquette discussed with us how he perceives a manager most effectively uses strategy within the game, "A lot of it is when to remove a starter or when to allow them to go a little bit deeper in the game. They have to determine a lot of times when they're tired. There are advanced metrics that you can use too but there's always a fine line for when to use the relievers and what kind of match ups to do, what kind of situations and circumstances. Sometimes you can develop a young pitcher into a key situation in the game based on your management skills, your leadership ability as a skipper."

A great example of a company that has exceeded with strategy is Starbucks. Their success has stemmed from great market segmentation, flawless execution, and outstanding leadership – we have already mentioned Howard Schultz several times but this is another example of how exemplary leadership propels an organization's success. Ron Roenicke, manager of the Milwaukee Brewers, talked with us about strategy in Major League Baseball, particularly from the manager's perspective. He said, "I think when you look at game strategy, in every game you play, so 162 games, and strategy wise, how many games a manager actually wins you by moves he makes? And it's more than one or two. But it's not a high number; it's not a 25 number. But you definitely make a difference on wins and losses by just strategy."

Results are What We Achieve

So we have our culture, our vision, and our strategy – but unless we can pull it all together to achieve our goals, we will not be successful. It comes down to the results we attain. That's what people view at the end of the year – profit margins, the win/loss column, and other predetermined metrics for your organization. Winning cultures are results-driven. These cultures are never satisfied with the status quo and they often tend to be customer-centric and extremely innovative. The leaders of these organizations have high levels of integrity and are seen as trusted leaders because they walk the talk every single day. Thus, truly winning cultures bring together a focus on results plus meaningful relationships. They use this synergy and a burning desire to achieve the organization's vision to maintain high standards. Much of this is accomplished because every member of the team views him/herself as an owner and takes personal responsibility for the overall results.

I find that I push more, and a little bit harder when

we're winning, than I do when we're losing.
Bob Melvin, manager, Oakland A's

In addition to having that burning desire to win, you must also believe that you can win. When an organization or a team has struggled for a length of time or perhaps they don't believe they have all the necessary resources, they may doubt that they have the ability to achieve their vision. Leadership plays a great part in closing the vision to reality gap and sometimes we just need to get a few small wins to help our team see that the bigger wins are a possibility. Bob Melvin talked about this and the effect of momentum and believing: "There are so many instances of teams that aren't picked to do anything, that get off to good starts and can get that team feeling and that winning feeling going that carries throughout the year, like the Diamond Backs last year [2011]. Arizona last year started out really poorly and then they went into a stretch where they had some success and they started believing. That momentum started to snowball for them and they started believing and they ended up doing what they did, so I think momentum in baseball is huge; optimism, belief, and belief in your team. If you have 25 guys with the same goal in mind, that's more powerful than when you have 3 or 4 guys that you're relying on. If you can really create that team unity, that's the most important thing, I think that's a very powerful thing."

As important as the leader is, we must also build a team where everyone is a leader – where everyone feels they are an owner in the organization and that they each take personal responsibility in seeing that the team achieves its goals. Brad Mills noted that, "most of them, they want to have success themselves, as well [wanting] the team to have success. If we can get them to be committed to that end, it sure makes it work a lot better." You must count on leaders within the ranks to take the reins and help to lead the team. These same individuals can also assist with accountability, standards, and even apply peer pressure towards performance results. This helps bring forward employee engagement and builds ownership in the vision. John Farrell discussed how a couple of his players really contributed in this manner. Farrell shared, "You know, we're fortunate that two of our best players are our leaders, Jose Bautista and Ricky Romero, one on both sides of the game - an everyday player and a pitcher. I can go to him [Jose Bautista] because he's an extremely intelligent and aware guy in his own right and he'll be able to articulate the pulse of what's happening within, what might be disrupting a group, or an issue that might be unresolved that needs to be addressed more directly. So yeah, they can handle a lot. We're fortunate, we have a group that somewhat polices themselves, but yet, under the notion that this is what we're about, this is what our goal is, this is what our vision is. So by no means is it a dictatorship. It can't be."

At our core, we want to succeed; to be number one; to earn the spotlight and accolades of our peers. In business, that may include being recognized in your community or in your industry. You might even aspire to receive national recognition such as the J.D. Power Awards in the automotive industry, Fortune's 100 Best Companies to Work For (Great Place to Work), or the

Malcolm Baldrige National Quality Award, to name a few. In Major League Baseball, it may start out wanting to win your division or perhaps a pennant but in reality, every team and every player truly wants to win the World Series Championship. And why not us? Maybe this is our year! We must have the vision and the desire to execute the plan to realize our greatest dreams.

Start Building Your Winning Culture

The true message in this chapter is that we must practice all of the leadership qualities discussed within this book in order to create a truly winning culture. Because culture is a pattern of dynamic relationships dependent upon the beliefs and attitudes of the organization's members, it is extremely complex yet simple at the same time. It is what we value – what we believe – what we do. It often starts with a dream or a vision of where we want to be in the future and this dream is inspired by our passion. Our vision, or destination, gives us a target in the future and a way to call upon the hopes and dreams of everyone in the organization. Once we have defined our vision we can begin to develop our strategy and goals (the roadmap) to direct us toward our destination. Ultimately, it is the results that we are able to achieve that determine our true success. But what can you do to build a winning culture with your organization, your department, or your team?

First, you will need to audit the existing culture to determine what is great about it, what is lacking, and what is unique about the organization. This is typically referred to as a culture audit. Next, define three to four primary values and guiding principles that truly define who you are as an organization. There must be a strong belief in these values because they will guide decisions within the organization. In addition, these values must be incorporated into the organization's performance management and reward systems because people pay attention to what is measured and what is recognized. Ensure the leadership team is completely on board with the values, culture, and overall direction. This values alignment may require a retreat or some form of a leadership development process to emphasize the importance of maintaining congruency between values and behaviors. To maintain momentum in this process, take time to communicate frequently and celebrate progress and success.

Your culture will predicate the decision making and behaviors within your organization. Take time to ensure the culture is where it needs to be to accomplish your goals and achieve your vision. Don't allow your culture to eat your strategy; instead, ensure it feeds it and strengthens it.

A trip to the mound...

- How would I describe the culture of my organization?
- Does our vision create excitement about the future?
- In what ways does our strategy create a roadmap to achieve our vision?
- What can I do to more effectively measure our results?
- Does our culture eat our strategy or feed and strengthen it?

Postgame:
Game Highlights

"I firmly believe that players win games and it's my job to put them in a situation where they'll be successful and if I do that then I'm doing a good job."

Davey Johnson, manager, Washington Nationals

"And that's the ballgame, folks!"

We've sat in the dugout, rounded the bases, and explored what it takes to win *your* game and achieve success with *your* team, so let's take a few moments to review the game highlights and how you can apply the ten *Bases of Major League Leadership* in your life.

> **It's been a little underrated in my opinion, what the manager's impact can be on the everyday lineup.**
>
> **Jim Duquette, Former MLB Executive, Sirius/XM Radio Personality**

The Happy Recap

Major League Leadership, as we've explored, is comprised of three dimensions of leadership, leading ourselves, leading others, and leading our game. In Part One we concluded that before we can lead others we must first learn to lead ourselves with a focus on inward reflection and insight, attributes that are critical in cultivating *Major League Leadership*. Before we can leave the dugout and work with our team we need to first consider **Finding our Passion** and have a game plan as to how we can best express it to our people, inspiring them to get engaged and become passionate as well. As we've explored, being a leader takes time, commitment, and energy, and without passion it is difficult to project optimism and excitement each day. Once we are in a position where we are passionate about what we are doing and are ready to lead our team, we then need to head out to the pitcher's mound, remembering that all eyes are on us, we are expected to set the tone of the game and **Lead by Example**. People are looking to us to see how we react in situations and to see what we do when we believe no one is watching. Our actions establish the norms and the culture of our organization and everyone expects us to be true to our words. With passion and leading by example understood, we now stroll to just behind home plate where the catcher resides. One of the things we must do as effective leaders is to be true to ourselves and true to the mission of our organization. When we do this we present an aura of respect for those around us and help establish trust amongst those we are leading. The catcher and the pitcher in a baseball game need to work together, trusting and respecting each other's expertise. As a leader, we need to **Earn Respect** from our people, and return it to them as well; it's a give and take that occurs each day. Remember what Davey Johnson said, no matter how long you've been in the game you need to gain trust and respect daily. This is true in whatever business we are in ... without trust those around us will not follow for long.

Now that we understand how to lead ourselves so that we can in turn lead others, let's take a tour of the proverbial infield and look at how we can lead others to achieve their potential. Let's imagine the infield, first base, second base, third base, and shortstop. In the infield, we focus on leading others, as there are many players who are a part the decisions we need to make. We need to run ninety feet from home plate to first base upon hitting the ball, but it often seems that the journey is longer when trying to beat the throw to first. The same can be said about leadership and our *Base*, **Know Your People**; what seems like a simple activity can sometimes feel like a never ending journey. We need to remind ourselves, like many of the managers we spoke with told us, that everyone is different, yet everyone deserves to be given the same respect and opportunity to excel. As a leader, finding this balance of personalization while maintaining fairness and consistency can be a challenge. Once we round that important *Base of Leadership,* we are now ready to go from first base to second base, as our next *base* is another ninety feet away. The first step in leading others is getting to know them; the second is to **Cultivate Relationships** with them so that they will want to perform for us. As we know, building relationships takes time, and this is something leaders are often short on. A simple conversation about how the other person spends his or her time off is a good way to begin this process. Finding commonalities with others often helps the relationship to develop and in turn breaks down barriers and also opens lines of communication.

Stretching the single to a double, and moving from *knowing our people* to *cultivating relationships* is great, but we can do more as leaders. By using our leadership skills we can push for a triple and get us that much closer to scoring a run. Another ninety feet, and we go to the next leadership necessity, we need to **Support our People.** Players (employees) need to believe that their manager has their back and will stand up for them at critical times. Understanding this gives them the freedom to work to the best of their ability without fear and it also builds confidence as well as loyalty. As you can see, the bases in this chapter all work together, and the last one for Part Two is what makes the other three effective, **Communicate Effectively.** The final position on the infield is that of short stop – the role on the field that often works with other players to get the out or even turn the double play – and this fits with our next *Base of Leadership, Communicate Effectively.* The ability to communicate can separate good leaders from great leaders as it can help limit embarrassing missteps while improving overall team effectiveness. When a leader is able to communicate his or her vision, inspire the others on the team to commit to it, and engage the team to work towards it, success will follow. At the conclusion of Part Two we know how to lead ourselves and lead others, and next we head to tour the outfield and discuss the nuts and bolts, the X's and O's of the game.

The outfielders have a lot of ground to cover, much like running a ballclub or business. Although the personal and people components of leadership are important, leaders will always have the responsibility of leading the game (running the business) as well, and need to focus on doing this most effectively. In revisiting our outfield, we start in left field and with the *Base,* **Know Your Game**. Great charisma can inspire an audience, but it cannot sustain any level of commitment if people do not find the leader to be credible. Effective leaders truly understand their business, their industry, and their customers. Although you should surround yourself with outstanding experts in each area, you must remain up to date on industry trends so your people will view you as a highly credible leader. Moving to our next position, centerfield, we focus on our *Base,* **Foster Teamwork**. In baseball the centerfielder is the leader of the outfield, he sets the tone and let's those around him know when to make a play or when to back off. A manager's job is to make sure that messages are delivered clearly, and from the right person, and the centerfielder does just that. The last position on the field is right field and that's where we are able to *Create a Winning Culture*. With the bases covered, we can focus on our ultimate goal – success – winning! As a leader, you must have the vision for the future and the ability to use your passion and knowledge to communicate it so that all members of the team share and embrace it. Your daily actions and interactions create the culture and establish the team's ability to reach its destination.

You are the leader, whether you wanted to be the leader or not, you're the leader and you have to make certain decisions.

Bud Harrelson, former manager, New York Mets

The Wrap Up

So that's a wrap, this game is over! However, remember, you will play again tomorrow and now is the time to start preparations and continue your development to be the best you can be and achieve your goals. Just as a pitcher can't throw a no-hitter without great defense behind him, the *Bases of Major League Leadership* will not work alone to bring about a win. The manager, the coaches, and the team as a whole must work together much like our winning strategies complement each other to bring about success on and off the field. Dive back into *Lead Me Out to the Ballgame*, review your notes, and use the tools we have explored to develop your *Major League Leadership* today.

Ten Bases of Major League Leadership

Lead Me Out to the Ballgame Roster[10]

Name	Position	Team[11]
Acta, Manny	**Manager**	**Cleveland Indians**
Atchison, Scott	Pitcher	Boston Red Sox
Aviles, Mike	Infielder	Boston Red Sox
Badenhop, Burke	Pitcher	Tampa Bay Rays
Bailey, Andrew	Pitcher	Boston Red Sox
Barmes, Clint	Infielder	Pittsburgh Pirates
Bautista, Jose	Outfielder	Toronto Blue Jays
Baylor, Don[12]	**Coach**	**Arizona Diamondbacks**
Black, Bud	**Manager**	**San Diego Padres**
Bloomquist, Willie	Infielder	Arizona Diamondbacks
Boswell, Thomas	Media	Washington Post
Breslow, Craig	Pitcher	Arizona Diamondbacks
Brignac, Reid	Infielder	Tampa Bay Rays
Brothers, Rex	Pitcher	Colorado Rockies
Broxton, Jonathan	Pitcher	Kansas City Royals
Burnett, Sean	Pitcher	Los Angeles Angels
Burnett, Sean	Pitcher	Washington Nationals
Burroughs, Sean	Infielder	Minnesota Twins

[10] Bold type indicates managerial experience at the Major League Level
[11] Team at time of interview
[12] Manager, Chicago Cubs 2000-2002 and Colorado Rockies 1993-1998

Name	Position	Team
Carpenter, Chris	Pitcher	Boston Red Sox
Carroll, Jamey	Infielder	Minnesota Twins
Chatwood, Tyler	Pitcher	Colorado Rockies
Chen, Bruce	Pitcher	Kansas City Royals
Clippard, Tyler	Pitcher	Washington Nationals
Coleman, Louis	Pitcher	Kansas City Royals
Coward, Kaleb	Infielder	Los Angeles Angels
Crow, Aaron	Pitcher	Kansas City Royals
DeRosa, Mark	Outfielder	Washington Nationals
Donaldson, Josh	Catcher	Oakland Athletics
Doumit, Ryan	Catcher	Minnesota Twins
Duke, Zach	Pitcher	Houston Astros
Dumatrait, Phil	Pitcher	Minnesota Twins
Duquette, Jim	Media	Sirius/XM Radio
Edlefsen, Steve	Pitcher	San Francisco Giants
Espinoza, Danny	Infielder	Washington Nationals
Farnsworth, Kyle	Pitcher	Tampa Bay Rays
Farrell, John	**Manager**	**Toronto Blue Jays**
Ferrin, Mike	Media	Sirius/XM Radio
Francis, Jeff	Pitcher	Colorado Rockies
Frasor, Jason	Pitcher	Toronto Blue Jays
Gardenhire, Ron	**Manager**	**Minnesota Twins**
Getz, Chris	Infielder	Kansas City Royals

Name	Position	Team
Gonzalez, Gio	Pitcher	Washington Nationals
Gorzelanny, Tom	Pitcher	Milwaukee Brewers
Guyer, Brandon	Outfielder	Tampa Bay Rays
Harper, Bryce	Outfielder	Washington Nationals
Harrelson, Bud[13]	**Co-owner/Coach**	**Long Island Ducks**
Helton, Todd	Infielder	Colorado Rockies
Hester, John	Catcher	Los Angeles Angels
Heston, Chris	Pitcher	San Francisco Giants
Hosmer, Eric	Infielder	Kansas City Royals
Hunsicker, Gerry	Executive VP	Tampa Bay Rays
Hurdle, Clint	**Manager**	**Pittsburgh Pirates**
Iannetta, Chris	Catcher	Los Angeles Angels
Johnson, Davey	**Manager**	**Washington Nationals**
Johnson, Howard	Coach	Seattle Mariners
Joyce, Matt	Outfielder	Tampa Bay Rays
Kalish, Ryan	Outfielder	Boston Red Sox
Kendrick, Howie	Infielder	Los Angeles Angels
Keppinger, Jeff	Infielder	Tampa Bay Rays
LaRoche, Adam	Infielder	Washington Nationals
Lidge, Brad	Pitcher	Washington Nationals
Lowrie, Jed	Infielder	Houston Astros

[13] Manager, New York Mets, 1990-1991

Name	Position	Team
Lyon, Brandon	Pitcher	Houston Astros
Maddon, Joe	**Manager**	**Tampa Bay Rays**
Magnuson, Trystan	Pitcher	Toronto Blue Jays
Manship, Jeff	Pitcher	Minnesota Twins
Marquis, Jason	Pitcher	Minnesota Twins
Mastroianni, Darin	Outfielder	Minnesota Twins
Mattingly, Don	**Manager**	**LA Dodgers**
Mauer, Joe	Catcher	Minnesota Twins
McCoy, Mike	Infielder	Toronto Blue Jays
Melvin, Bob	**Manager**	**Oakland Athletics**
Michaels, Jason	Outfielder	Washington Nationals
Mills, Brad	**Manager**	**Houston Astros**
Miner, Zach	Pitcher	Kansas City Royals
Moore, Scott	Infielder	Houston Astros
Morris, Bryan	Pitcher	Pittsburgh Pirates
Norris, Bud	Pitcher	Houston Astros
Oliva, Tony	Retired	Minnesota Twins
Oliver, Darren	Pitcher	Toronto Blue Jays
Ortiz, David	DH	Boston Red Sox
Otero, Dan	Pitcher	San Francisco Giants
Overbay, Lyle	Infielder	Arizona Diamondbacks
Pavano, Carl	Pitcher	Minnesota Twins
Pence, Hunter	Outfielder	San Francisco Giants

Name	Position	Team
Prince, Josh	Outfielder	Milwaukee Brewers
Ransom, Cody	Infielder	Arizona Diamondbacks
Rhymes, Will	Infielder	Tampa Bay Rays
Robinson, Clint	Infielder	Kansas City Royals
Roenicke, Ron	**Manager**	**Milwaukee Brewers**
Romero, Ricky	Pitcher	Toronto Blue Jays
Romine, Andrew	Infielder	Los Angeles Angels
Ryan, Terry	General Manager	Minnesota Twins
Saltalamacchia, Jarrod	Catcher	Boston Red Sox
Sandoval, Pablo	Infielder	San Francisco Giants
Schafer, Logan	Outfielder	Milwaukee Brewers
Schlichting, Travis	Pitcher	Oakland Athletics
Scioscia, Mike	**Manager**	**Los Angeles Angels**
Sinatro, Matt	Coach	Houston Astros
Snyder, Chris	Catcher	Houston Astros
Sweeney, Ryan	Outfielder	Boston Red Sox
Taubensee, Eddie	Retired	
Taylor, Michael	Outfielder	Oakland Athletics
Thames, Eric	Outfielder	Toronto Blue Jays
Thurston, Joe	Utility	Houston Astros
Towles, JR	Catcher	Minnesota Twins
Tracy, Chad	Infielder	Washington Nationals

Name	Position	Team
Trammell, Alan[14]	**Coach**	**Arizona Diamondbacks**
Trout, Mike	Outfielder	Los Angeles Angels
Upton, BJ	Outfielder	Tampa Bay Rays
Vizquel, Omar	Infielder	Toronto Blue Jays
Vogelsong, Ryan	Pitcher	San Francisco Giants
Wagner, Neil	Pitcher	Oakland Athletics
Washington, Ron	**Manager**	**Texas Rangers**
Weeks, Rickie	Infielder	Milwaukee Brewers
Weiland, Kyle	Pitcher	Houston Astros
Wells, Casper	Outfielder	Seattle Mariners
Wooten, Sean	Coach	Los Angeles Dodgers
Wheeler, Ryan	Infielder	Colorado Rockies
Willingham, Josh	Outfielder	Minnesota Twins
Yost, Ned	**Manager**	**Kansas City Royals**
Ziegler, Brad	Pitcher	Arizona Diamondbacks

[14] Manager, Detroit Tigers, 2002 - 2005

Notes

1 Walter, E. 50 Heavyweight Leadership Quotes. Forbes. Retrieved from http://www.forbes.com/sites/ekaterinawalter/2013/09/30/50-heavyweight-leadership-quotes/

2 Crowley, M. *Lead From the Heart.* Retrieved from http://markccrowley.com/four-great -examples-of-how-starbucks-howard-schultz-leads-from-the-heart/#sthash.1q88xNrN.dpbs

3 Kouzes, J., & Posner, B. (2008). *The Leadership Challenge, 4th Edition.* Jossey Bass.

4 Wooden, J., & Jamison, S. (2005). *Wooden on Leadership.* New York: McGraw-Hill. (p.20)

5 Wooden, J., & Jamison, S. (2005). *Wooden on Leadership.* New York: McGraw-Hill. (p. 33)

6 Perkins, D.T. & Murphy, J.B. (2013). *Into the Storm: Lessons in Teamwork from the Treacherous Sydney to Hobart Ocean Race.* New York: Amacom.

7 Goleman, D. (2008). *Emotional intelligence: 10th anniversary edition; why it can matter more than IQ* (10 ed.). New York: Bantam.

8 Wooden, J., & Jamison, S. (2005). *Wooden on Leadership.* New York: McGraw-Hill. (p. 98)

9 Collins, J. Good to Great. Retrieved from http://www.jimcollins.com/article_topics/articles /good-to-great.html

10 Ladson, B. *Nats deal Carroll to Rockies.* Washington Nationals.com. Retrieved from http://washington.nationals.mlb.com/news/article.jsp?ymd=20060211&content_id =1310107&vkey=news_was&fext=.jsp&c_id=was

11 Peter F. Drucker quotes. Thinkexist.com. Retrieved from http://thinkexist.com/quotation/ management_is_doing_things_right-leadership_is/11721.html

12 http://thegoodinsports.com/athlete-charity-directory/pg/1/?cn-cat=2

13 Rainmaker Thinking, Inc. www.rainmakerthinking.com

14 Peters, T.J. & Waterman, R.H. (1982). In Search of Excellence, Lessons from America's Best-Run Companies. New York: Harper & Row.

15 Goleman, D. (2008). *Emotional intelligence: 10th anniversary edition; why it can matter more than IQ.* (10 ed.). New York, NY: Bantam.

16 Donne, J. (1624). *Meditation XVII.* Retrieved from http://www.online-literature.com/ donne/409/

17 The single biggest problem in communication is the illusion that it has taken place. Philosiblog. Retrieved from

http://philosiblog.com/2012/01/06/the-single-biggest-problem-in-communication-is-the-illusion-that-it-has-taken-place/

[18] Hall of Fame Speech - June 12, 1939. Babe Ruth. Retrieved from http://www.baberuth.com/quotes/

[19] Zappos.com Powered by Service. Zappos Family Core Values. Retrieved from http://about.zappos.com/our-unique-culture/zappos-core-values

[20] Southwest Airlines. Culture. Southwest Airlines Careers. Retrieved from http://www.southwest.com/html/about-southwest/careers/culture.html

Index

About the Authors

Howard C. Fero, Ph.D, *The Leadership Doc*, is a leadership speaker, professor, consultant, and executive coach. He is a sought after speaker and has been recognized as an 'inspirational, motivational, and innovative facilitator'. Dr. Fero works with individuals and groups helping them to cultivate their leadership, identify and focus their motivation, and create high performing teams. He is the Director of Graduate Leadership Programs and an Associate Professor of Management and Leadership at Albertus Magnus College in New Haven, CT, and was recently recognized as a *Business New Haven Rising Star*. Dr. Fero lives with his three children and wife, interior designer, Lisa Fero, in Connecticut. He holds a Master's degree in Industrial and Organizational Psychology from Baruch College, the City University of New York, and a Ph.D in Organizational Behavior from Claremont Graduate University. For more information please go to www.TheLeadershipDoc.com.

Rebecca L. Herman, Ph.D, is a leadership professor, transformational speaker, passionate volunteer leader, baseball blogger, and avid photographer. She loves to work with people to help them achieve their fullest potential. Dr. Herman is a Professor of Leadership and Organizational Development for Kaplan University's School of Business graduate programs. Prior to her academic

appointment, Dr. Herman enjoyed a successful career as a leader in Human Resources for over two decades. She is a member of Alpha Omicron Pi fraternity with over 30 years of volunteer service and is currently serving as International Vice President on the Executive Board. Dr. Herman lives with her son in San Diego, CA. She holds a Master's degree in Organizational Management from the University of Phoenix, a Ph.D in Organization & Management from Capella University and is certified as a Senior Professional in Human Resources (SPHR). For more information, please visit www.RebeccaHermanPhd.com.

To learn more about developing your

Major League Leadership

or to invite

Dr. Howard Fero

or

Dr. Rebecca Herman

to speak at your next event

please head to

www.MajorLeagueLeadership.com

Made in the USA
Charleston, SC
09 May 2014